Awakening the
SLEEPING
GIANT

THIRD EDITION

Awakening the SLEEPING GIANT

THIRD EDITION

Helping Teachers Develop as Leaders

Marilyn Katzenmeyer
Gayle Moller

CORWIN
A SAGE Company

For information:

Corwin
A SAGE Company
2455 Teller Road
Thousand Oaks, California 91320
(800) 233-9936
Fax: (800) 417-2466
www.corwinpress.com

SAGE Ltd.
1 Oliver's Yard
55 City Road
London EC1Y 1SP
United Kingdom

SAGE India Pvt. Ltd.
B 1/I 1 Mohan Cooperative
    Industrial Area
Mathura Road, New Delhi 110 044
India

SAGE Asia-Pacific Pte. Ltd.
33 Pekin Street #02-01
Far East Square
Singapore 048763

Printed in the United States of America.

Library of Congress Cataloging-in-Publication Data

Katzenmeyer, Marilyn.
    Awakening the sleeping giant: Helping teachers develop as leaders / Marilyn Katzenmeyer, Gayle Moller.—3rd ed.
        p. cm.
    Includes bibliographical references and index.
    ISBN 978-1-4129-6039-7 (cloth)
    ISBN 978-1-4129-6040-3 (pbk.)
        1. Teachers—Training of—United States. 2. Educational leadership—United States. 3. Teachers—In-service training—United States. I. Moller, Gayle. II. Title.

LB1715.K28 2009
370.71'55—dc21   2009002808

This book is printed on acid-free paper.

        10 11 12 13   10 9 8 7 6 5 4 3

Acquisitions Editor:	Dan Alpert
Associate Editor:	Megan Bedell
Associate Editor:	Desirée A. Bartlett
Production Editor:	Libby Larson
Copy Editor:	Cate Huisman
Typesetter:	C&M Digitals (P) Ltd.
Proofreader:	Wendy Jo Dymond
Indexer:	Terri Corry
Cover and Graphic Designer:	Scott Van Atta

Contents

Preface

This book focuses on teachers as leaders and the importance of teacher leadership to improved outcomes in our schools. America's schools draw vitality from the creativity and commitment of their teachers. Teachers, the largest group of potential adult leaders in schools, hold the most promise for unlimited contributions to school change. The efforts of dedicated, talented teachers have always provided the energy needed to make schools sensitive to the needs of each generation of students.

Dramatic changes in the world and the increased pressures placed on schools to support the nation's economy create a context that makes it impossible to respond as we have in the past. Facing the increasing pressures of testing and more accountability, schools experiment with a multitude of change efforts, and still the media, the public, and even educators bemoan our schools' inadequate progress in meeting the needs of all of our students. Neither legislative mandates, nor central office directives, nor principal-initiated projects will result in the major change needed. There is clearly, however, hope through increased opportunities for teachers serving as instructional leaders and assuming other leadership functions to move our educational systems toward meeting expectations that have thus far been unfulfilled. In fact, Melissa Rasberry, a colleague at the Center for Teaching Quality, said, "The stars are aligning for teacher leadership," and indeed they are.

Our experience with teacher leaders reveals that they are already making a difference in teaching and learning in many schools. It is out of this experience that we recognize the critical nature of the role that teacher leaders must play if visions and hopes for schools are to be realized. Teacher leaders provide the key to sustaining meaningful change in schools. As part of our work over the years, we attempted to identify the knowledge and skills that are characteristic of outstanding teacher leaders. Once these were identified, we realized that little of the knowledge and few of the skills are taught in most teacher preparation programs. Also, inadequate attention is given to teacher leadership development within schools and districts. Further, the structure and norms within schools and the lack of understanding among principals, superintendents, and district staff often inhibit the emergence of teacher leadership. To address this need, we focused our efforts on the development needs of teacher leaders. By relying on the knowledge acquired throughout our careers in school reform and by acknowledging the leadership of which teachers are capable, we strengthened our belief in the power of teacher leadership to make a difference.

In this third edition, we share our experience and the insights gained over the past two decades of studying and observing the work of teacher leaders. We add to our definition of teacher leadership and include new content related to the evolution of teacher leadership since the second edition was written. We offer thoughts on promoting teacher leadership. We include our recent thinking on the career-long development of teacher leaders, beginning with preservice preparation programs and continuing through to ongoing support for experienced teacher leaders. New content focuses on the implications of generational differences among faculty members and offers clues to building relationships with those who bring diverse perspectives to the workplace. The school context for supporting teacher leadership is analyzed, and we offer a set of dimensions evident in schools where teacher leadership is thriving. We share three factors critical to sustaining teacher leadership in schools, including (1) the relationships among adults in the school, (2) the school's organizational structure, and (3) the actions of the principal. In this edition, we provide more fully developed ideas on steps for teacher leaders to take in influencing colleagues, their schools, and their districts. Focusing on the vast numbers of teachers now serving as instructional leaders, we acquaint readers of this new edition with timely, new content related to the four challenges many teacher leaders face: deciding to accept a leadership role, building principal–teacher leader relationships, working with peers, and facilitating professional learning for self and others. Finally, we disclose our thinking about teacher leadership in the future, including areas for advocacy and change to assure that future is a positive one.

The third edition contains updated references from teacher leadership literature and research throughout each chapter. The content is further enhanced by the inclusion of two new instruments, the Teacher Leadership Self-Assessment and the Teacher Leadership School Survey. Other instruments provided include the Readiness for Teacher Leadership Survey and the Philosophy of Education Inventory. These instruments offer readers unique measures that can be used by potential and practicing teacher leaders. In addition, new print and online resources are provided to aid those who wish to study teacher leadership in greater depth.

We are pleased that there is a growing trend to honor teacher leadership and to build teachers' leadership skills, because we wrote the first edition of this book in hope of awakening this sleeping giant over a decade ago. This book will benefit all those interested in understanding the power of teacher leadership and in helping teachers develop as leaders. The responsibility for advocating teacher leadership falls on the shoulders of people in diverse roles, including principals, superintendents, district staff, college and university personnel, and especially teachers themselves. We need the attention of all these groups. In this third edition, we have reexamined the teacher leadership beliefs we have held and matched these beliefs with our more recent experiences. Our ideas are, as always, guided by our interactions with teacher leaders around the country. In this third edition, we share what we have learned about teacher leadership with those who wish to capitalize on this vital resource.

The journey of developing teachers as leaders is one that we have been on throughout our careers. It is our hope that everyone with a stake in assuring success for all students in our nation's schools will join us on this journey and that the ideas proposed in this book will be helpful to all of you.

Acknowledgments

As we worked on the third edition of this book, we were reminded of teacher leaders who inspired us over the last 20 years. There are thousands of teacher leaders who work tirelessly to make a difference in the lives of their students. Our interactions with many of these individuals enriched our lives and influenced our writing.

At this stage of our careers, we are grateful for the encouragement of people who feel as deeply as we do about teacher leadership. These leaders include Roland Barth, Gordy Donaldson, Bill Drummond, Betty Epanchin, Cecil Golden, Shirley Hord, and Linda Lambert. In addition, there are outstanding educators who are leaders of teacher leaders. Linda Diaz, Regina Ash, Debra Elliott, Betsy Burrows, Scott Elliott, Martha Harrill, Pam Houfek, Janet Mason, Renee Coward, and Todd Cluff are examples of these leaders who have touched our lives.

In recent years, the rich conversations of the members of the Teacher Leaders Network (TLN) informed and inspired our work. John Norton, the tireless facilitator of the TLN, deserves special recognition for his ongoing support of these teacher leaders. Barnett Berry, president and CEO of the Center for Teaching Quality, works passionately to find resources to continue the work of the TLN and other initiatives that promote teacher leadership.

Finally, we appreciate the patience and encouragement of our families while we made sense of our experiences with teacher leaders and their leadership. We especially acknowledge the support of our husbands, Bill Katzenmeyer and Jim Moller, two educational leaders themselves.

Marilyn Katzenmeyer

Gayle Moller

Corwin gratefully acknowledges the contributions of the following reviewers:

Melanie Mares, Academic Coach
Lowndes Middle School, Valdosta, GA

Thomas McGuire, Professor
University of La Verne, CA

Lauren Mittermann, Seventh and Eighth Grade
    Social Studies Teacher
Gibraltar Middle School, Fish Creek, WI

Susan H. Moody, Language Arts Teacher
William Penn High School, New Castle, DE

Joan Taylor, Title I Coordinator
Washoe County School District, Reno, NV

About the Authors

Marilyn Katzenmeyer is president of Professional Development Center, Incorporated, and she currently engages in consultation, instructional design, and professional writing. She most recently served as a faculty administrator at the University of South Florida, where she was responsible for the development and implementation of the Executive Leaders Program, a leadership development opportunity for school-based administrators and teacher leaders who were transitioning into district-level leadership roles, and for the coordination of a Transition to Teaching project with a local school district. She was formerly executive director of the West Central Educational Leadership Network, which provided leadership training and school improvement assistance to educators throughout 13 school districts in southwest Florida. She has been a human resource development professional throughout her career, and she was the first director of the Broward County School District (Fort Lauderdale, Florida) Human Resource Development Department. Marilyn worked in Ohio and Florida as a secondary school teacher. She received her doctorate in adult education from Florida State University. Her research focused on effective strategies for measuring the impact of leadership training programs on the behavior of school administrators. Marilyn and her husband, Bill, divide their time between Tampa, Florida, and the mountains of northern Georgia.

Gayle Moller recently retired as associate professor in the Department of Educational Leadership and Foundations at Western Carolina University in Cullowhee, North Carolina. She was formerly executive director of the South Florida Center for Educational Leaders. The center served large, urban school systems in South Florida that provided staff development for school leaders. Gayle worked in the Broward County Public Schools (Fort Lauderdale, Florida) for 19 years as a teacher, school administrator, and staff development administrator. Gayle received her doctorate from Teachers College/Columbia University. Teacher leadership and professional learning communities are her research interests. Gayle served on the board of trustees of the National Staff Development Council. She is a coauthor, with Anita Pankake, of *Lead With Me: A Principal's Guide to Teacher Leadership*. Gayle and her husband, Jim, live in Franklin, North Carolina.

1

Understanding Teacher Leadership

Being a teacher leader means sharing and representing relevant and key ideas of our work as teachers in contexts beyond our individual classrooms so as to improve the education of our students and our ability to provide it for them.

Ariel Sacks, Eighth Grade Teacher Leader

Hardworking educators struggle every day within a system that was not designed for the needs of today's students. In spite of the skepticism of the public and the ensuing policy reports that reveal failures within our educational system, most teachers are committed to searching for answers to improve student outcomes, although other demands compete for their attention. The unending need to find social services for students and their families, competitive challenges from advocates of charter schools and school vouchers, and the dwindling numbers of capable individuals who want to become teachers and school administrators create distractions from the challenge committed educators face in improving student learning.

Over the last 25 years, the massive number of reports on how to improve schools influenced policymakers to pass legislation placing pressure on educators to provide quality education for all students. Few would disagree with this goal. Many would argue, though, that the goal cannot be accomplished by simply raising standards, creating and implementing more outcome measures, and holding students, teachers, and administrators ever more accountable for test scores. Research on the impact of the accountability movement (Darling-Hammond & Prince, 2007; Wechsler et al., 2007) has helped us understand that investing in teachers and their learning, rather than creating more tests, is a better investment for improving student outcomes. Unlike well-intentioned policymakers who persist in their search for "silver bullet" legislation to reform schools, savvy parents already know that the focus of reform efforts should be on the classroom teacher, who can make the most difference in their children's learning.

After mixed results with accountability measures, externally designed reform programs, and reward/punishment systems meant to exact higher test scores, the focus is turning toward individual classrooms and teacher quality (*Education Week*, 2008). To improve teacher quality, teachers need to learn to teach better. So attention has shifted to professional development, formerly an occasional experience for most teachers that is now a frequent obligation for every teacher regardless of the relevance for the teacher. Vendors, district administrators, school reform leaders, and others provide menus of professional development; some reflect quality, but many violate even the rudimentary standards for effective professional development. Wechsler et al. (2007), in a study of teaching in California, reported that this state does not have a coherent approach to ensuring that teachers have the knowledge and skills to be effective, and this conclusion would most likely also be true in every state.

Perhaps the answers to concerns about education rest in the potential of a leadership structure that taps into everyone's talents within the school community, especially the teachers. There cannot be significant progress within an educational system in which hierarchical control separates managers (school principals) from workers (teachers). Leadership must be "embedded in the school community as a whole" (Lambert, 1998, p. 5). The notion of the principal as the only leader is evolving into a clearer understanding of the leadership roles that teachers must take if our schools are to be successful.

Within every school there is a *sleeping giant* of teacher leadership that can be a strong catalyst for making changes to improve student learning. By using the energy of teacher leaders as agents of school change, public education will stand a better chance of ensuring that "every child has a high quality teacher" (Wehling, 2007, p. 14). We can call upon the leadership of teachers—the largest group of school employees and those closest to the students—to ensure a high level of teacher quality by bringing their vast resources to bear on continuously improving the schools. By helping teachers recognize that they are leaders, by offering opportunities to develop their leadership skills, and by creating school cultures that honor their leadership, we can awaken this sleeping giant of teacher leadership.

In order to do this, we begin in this chapter to examine how teacher leadership emerged. Then we share our expanded definition of teacher leadership. To illustrate the definition, we provide three examples of teacher leaders who struggle with universal dilemmas teacher leaders face. We next invite teachers to assess their inclination to be teacher leaders using the Readiness for Teacher Leadership instrument. Finally, we suggest that everyone has a responsibility to support teacher leaders, because teacher leaders cannot do it alone within the existing system.

Teacher Leadership Emerges

When we wrote the first edition of this book in the mid-1990s, the concept of "teacher leadership" was relatively unknown. We discovered the importance of teacher leadership in our work with principals and school improvement. Principals who learned with teachers about school reform were more likely to transfer their learning from professional development workshops to the work in their schools. Unfortunately, though, many of the principals were transferred to other schools, and the initiatives at their previous schools fell to whims of the next principal. The teachers who had been colearners with their former principals were disillusioned and powerless to sustain their work. We wondered how systems could be built to sustain school improvement initiatives over time in spite of who sat in the principal's office. We dreamed that in every school, there would be a critical mass of positive teacher leaders who had the knowledge, skills, and beliefs to maintain the momentum of school improvement that influenced student learning. The gap between our dream for teacher leadership and the reality of school leadership structures has been an obstacle for over 20 years.

In spite of these obstacles, today, teacher leadership is emerging, and in many schools teacher leaders are finding their voices. Previously, if we asked a principal to identify teacher leaders, most often there were long hesitations and tentative responses; finally principals responded by identifying the textbook chairperson or the team leader. Yet they did not consider these teachers as "real" leaders, and certainly the teachers in those positions did not see themselves as leaders. Currently, "teacher leadership" is a more familiar term as evidenced by the vast growth of the numbers of instructional leadership positions, the inclusion of teacher leadership in standards for teachers, collaborative work across states on licensure for teacher leaders, and the proliferation of teacher leadership literature.

A primary reason that teacher leader positions are emerging is that school systems recognize that the professional development offered to teachers does not result in changed teacher behavior in the classroom unless follow-up coaching and support are offered. Teacher leaders with titles such as literacy coach, mentor, and lead teacher provide on-site assistance for teachers. As teachers take on leadership roles, they are uniting and reaching out beyond their classrooms to influence educational policy through professional networks, such as the Teacher Leaders Network (www.teacherleaders.org) that spans the United States.

Meanwhile, the number of journals, research reports, and books focused on teacher leadership is growing (Mangin & Stoelinga, 2008). We hear from many doctoral students who are engaged in writing dissertations that study teacher leadership and its impact. Although important first steps are underway, we look forward to the unleashing of leadership talent within every school as the norm.

To tap into the potential of teacher leadership requires moving beyond changing policy, enforcing mandates, and offering professional development. These reform strategies are relatively easy compared to the challenges of guaranteeing teacher quality in every classroom, ensuring effective principal leadership, and engaging teachers in meaningful leadership responsibilities. To reach these goals, we must overcome three obstacles. First, the structure of school and school system leadership must be examined. Next, there must be a shift from the old norms of teaching in isolation and focusing on just "my students." Finally, many teachers must recognize that a broader role of teacher leadership is open and available to those who wish to assume the responsibilities. Teaching is basically a "flat" profession (Danielson, 2007, p. 14), in which a teacher's responsibilities can remain the same from the first day of teaching until retirement regardless of the level of expertise gained over the years. Although many teachers engage in collaborative work and practice shared decision making to expand their circle of influence to *all* students and *all* teachers in *their* schools, too many teachers and administrators work in parallel universes, where formal leadership still rests in the principal's office and teacher leadership is haphazard at best.

While teacher leadership is no longer an unknown idea, it is "sometimes touted, but [it is] rarely fully realized" (Berry, Norton, & Byrd, 2007, p. 48). In our work with teacher leaders, we wondered why teachers are hesitant to be called leaders even when they are active in leadership activities. Regardless of the region of the country, we found three major reasons for their reluctance. First, the quality of teacher leadership depends on the culture of the school. Teachers describe school contexts that do not encourage them to be leaders. Often teachers who are motivated to become leaders will leave these unsupportive school cultures and will seek out schools more con-ducive to their leadership aspirations. A second concern is that teach-ers feel they do not have the skills to lead other adults. While principals and other leaders are required to learn leadership skills, teachers rarely are engaged in building these skills. Finally, the egali-tarian norms of school cultures suggest that all teachers should be equal. This strong norm discourages teachers from drawing attention to themselves. Fearing the reactions of their colleagues, teachers hes-itate to be singled out of the group in an environment that has valued treating all teachers the same (Johnson & Donaldson, 2007). All of these factors impede the progress of teacher leadership. As teacher leadership becomes more widely accepted in some schools, the cul-ture of teaching has more readily embraced leadership from peers (Mackenzie, 2007).

Teacher leadership is essential for the level of complex change schools face. In order to advance these roles for teachers, it is neces-sary for proponents to be clear about what teacher leadership is.

Definition of Teacher Leadership

There is common agreement that we are a long way from a wide-spread understanding of teacher leadership. Confusion about defini-tions and expectations of teacher leaders abound (York-Barr & Duke, 2004). Just what does teacher leadership look like? Who are teacher leaders? In the past, when we visited groups that were interested in teacher leadership, there was a request for time to clarify the concept of teacher leadership. Now we face a different predicament. Since teacher leadership is popular in the educator's professional jargon, there is a reluctance to examine the concept, because everyone believes he or she knows what it means. Regardless of the interest or lack of interest in defining teacher leadership, we believe a dialogue about the definition provides the foundation for a common understanding in order to promote and support teacher leaders.

We arrived at our definition of teacher leadership after a review of the educational literature, careful consideration of our experiences, and much conversation with teacher leaders, principals, and others. This definition continues to evolve as we continue our exploration and learning. Our definition is teachers leaders lead within and beyond the classroom; identify with and contribute to a community of teacher learners and leaders; influence others toward improved educational practice; and accept responsibility for achieving the outcomes of their leadership.

Lead Within and Beyond the Classroom

The professional teacher is first of all competent in the classroom through the facilitation of students' learning. Teacher leadership is allowed by other teachers when the teacher is perceived as a capable teacher of students. Little (1995) cited legitimacy for leadership as a prerequisite for teacher leaders in their influence of peers. This legitimacy can only be given by other teachers and not by a positional title. Teachers we meet clearly accept this part of the leadership role, and some even recognize that they can transfer many classroom skills to their work with peers. Teachers can be leaders of change beyond their classrooms by accepting more responsibility for helping colleagues to achieve success for all of the students and for the total school program.

The level of involvement in teacher leadership beyond the classroom depends on the context of the school and the school system as well as the teacher's willingness. Most important, teachers do not have to divorce themselves from focusing on teaching and learning to be leaders. In the past, a commonly held belief was that if you were a teacher, the only way to become a leader was to leave the classroom and possibly the school (Barth, 1988; Boyer, 1983). Few teachers are attracted to school administration, and if they prepare for this role, it is because administration appears to be their only option for affecting students more broadly. The goal of becoming an administrator as the only way of getting ahead in education is giving way to teachers finding other outlets for their leadership both inside and outside their schools.

There are differences of opinion about teachers becoming leaders by taking responsibilities outside classrooms they consider their own. When we first started working with teacher leadership, we advocated for teachers to continue to teach while contributing beyond the classroom. We feared that teacher leaders might lose their connection to the classroom. With the emerging formal roles for teacher leaders, such as those of math coach or full time mentor of new teachers, we acknowledge that teacher leaders may leave the classroom and remain quite effective in working with other teachers. Their work is still focused on the improvement of teaching and learning, but within their colleagues' classrooms. Time demands and increased workload make it difficult for some teacher leaders to remain full time in the classroom and also to take on demanding leadership roles. Formal teacher leader roles can enable teachers to be valuable contributors to school improvement as long as the teacher leaders are not pulled into quasi-administrative responsibilities that take them away from the focus on teaching and their authentic relationships with colleague teachers.

Leadership, of course, is not limited to a selected group of lead teachers or master teachers. Teachers who choose not to leave the classroom and instead to assume informal leadership roles within the school are equally valued and powerful. Drawing from their expertise and passion for teaching, these teachers influence other teachers informally through having casual conversations, sharing materials, facilitating professional development, or simply extending an invitation for other teachers to visit their classrooms.

Teacher leadership roles empower teachers to realize their professional worth while still maintaining the centrality of their teaching roles (Stone, Horejs, & Lomas, 1997). Although some teacher leaders may seek administrative roles, most teachers in leadership roles do not view these opportunities as steps up the ladder to the administrative ranks. These teachers want to remain close to students and are willing to assume leadership roles that will affect decisions related to their daily practice with those students.

Contribute to a Community of Learners and Leaders

Leading beyond the classroom provides an opportunity for teachers to interact with other adults in the school. Ackerman and Mackenzie (2007) suggested that teacher leaders "live for the dream of feeling part of a collective, collaborative enterprise" (p. 237). If this dream is realized, teachers learn within the school's professional community. Barth (2001) suggested that there is a "powerful relationship between learning and leading" (p. 445). Although the concept of professional learning communities emerged as a logical way to engage the adults in the school in their own learning, the realization of this type of school culture is relatively rare. Developing a professional learning community is more difficult than most people realize. Yet when teacher leaders do join a community of learners and leaders, in contrast to an elitist group, it opens up opportunities for every teacher to be a part of the community.

Teacher leaders, though, know the value of working with their peers in "communities of practice" (Lieberman & Miller, 2004, p. 22) or their own professional learning communities. Within these settings, teachers are learning in social context rather than only learning individually (Stein, Smith, & Silver, 1999). Teacher leadership develops naturally among professionals who learn, share, and address problems together.

When teacher leaders and principals expand professional learning communities to include the entire school, then all teachers are included in the professional learning. Hord's (2003) examination of professional learning communities reveals that teacher leaders are partners with the formal school leaders in their efforts to improve teaching and learning. Five dimensions emerge as attributes of schools that are professional learning communities. The dimensions are

1. Supportive and shared leadership: School administrators participate democratically with teachers—sharing power, authority, and decision making.

2. Shared values and vision: School administrators and teachers share visions for school improvement that have an undeviating focus on student learning and that are consistently referenced for the staff's work.

3. Collective learning and application of learning: Faculty and staff collective learning and application of the learning (taking action) create high intellectual learning tasks and solutions to address student needs.

4. Supportive conditions: School conditions and human capacities support the staff's arrangement as a professional learning organization.

5. Shared personal practice: Peers review and give feedback on teacher instructional practice in order to increase individual and organizational capacity. (Hord, 2003, p. 7)

Teacher leaders thrive in professional learning communities that exhibit these attributes. Credible teachers are empowered to assume leadership roles with the support of their peers. A critical mass of teacher leaders engaged in a professional learning community can often maintain momentum in a school's improvement efforts even during changes in formal, administrative leadership. The lack of continuity of leadership in schools and school districts makes maintaining reforms difficult (Fullan, 2005), but a professional learning community provides the best buffer we have to prevent this level of disturbance to sustainability of improvement efforts.

PLCs
capacity

Teacher leaders also reach outside their schools to a wider professional community. Participation in national educational projects, professional organizations, and other external school reform movements provide teachers with networks of other teacher leaders who reinforce improved teaching practices. Lieberman and Wood (2003) documented the value of teacher involvement in external networks. These communities of learners and leaders can be the impetus for teachers to realize that their leadership skills are valuable and can give them the courage to lead within their own school while developing both professional expertise and leadership skills.

Finally, teacher leaders know how to build alliances and networks in order to accomplish their work (Crowther, 2008). These connections help them to pull together the necessary people, funding, and other resources to support their action plans. They know the social dynamics within the school and how to connect like-minded people as well as work with the skeptics. Depending on the health of the school culture, teacher leaders can build community and collaboratively find ways to make a difference for students.

Influence Others Toward Improved Practice

Teacher leaders influence others toward improved educational practice. A key word in our notion of teacher leadership is *influence.* There is probably not another profession that provides more practice in influencing than teaching, in which students are influenced daily by their teachers. The art of transferring these skills into work with colleagues, although complex, can be learned by teacher leaders.

Leadership is influencing. Teacher leaders are approachable and influence primarily through their relationships, which become the foundation upon which teacher leaders are able to share and learn with others. Silva, Gimbert, and Nolan (2000) found in their study of teacher leaders that building relationships was critical in their work. Also, Mooney (1994) reported descriptions of teacher leaders by other teachers. Teacher leaders were described as hardworking, involved with innovation, motivating students with a variety of abilities, and available to other teachers.

Formal positions are not necessary to influence others. In fact, teachers collaborating with their colleagues are just as effective in influencing others as are individuals with formal titles who carry the power of a position (Lambert, 2003). Motivating colleagues toward improved practice relies on the personal influence of competent teachers who have positive relationships with other adults in the school. In every school there are teacher leaders who show initiative, willingly experiment with new ideas, and then share their experiences with others.

Colleagues are influenced if leaders exhibit behaviors they advocate. Teacher leaders may engage in "reaching out to others with encouragement, technical knowledge to solve classroom problems, and enthusiasm for learning new things" (Rosenholtz, 1989, p. 208). Successful teacher leaders we know are consummate learners who pay attention to their own development and model continuous learning. Sharing information and visibly improving their own practice gives teacher leaders endorsement in their work with other teachers. Teachers who are credible to their peers, who are continuous learners, and who pass relevant information about best practices to others influence their colleague teachers. While teacher leaders are working in professional communities, they are, in turn, influenced by other teachers.

This attribute of teacher leadership is the most difficult to accomplish within a teacher culture that does not easily acknowledge that a colleague may have knowledge to share. The delicate balance of relationships is a constant challenge for teacher leaders who want to influence others to work together toward the goal of improved practice. Unless this balance is achieved, teachers can remain isolated except to share "war stories" about their daily interactions with students, parents, and even administrators.

Accept Responsibility for Achieving Outcomes

Leadership assumes accountability for results. This is a new component in our definition, and when we have shared it with different groups of leaders, there has been universal agreement that taking responsibility for one's leadership is crucial for teacher leadership to be taken seriously. One teacher shared, "If we design the leadership role, we are also obligated to accept the accountability that comes with it." As a result of these kinds of conversations with teacher leaders, the definition is expanded to include this component.

Teachers often enter leadership roles by recognizing an area for improvement and then addressing the issue. This passion for finding solutions can lead to multiple and extensive ideas that require a high level of energy and more time than is available. For these reasons and many others, teachers can become discouraged and desert the plans midstream. In contrast, teacher leaders take responsibility for follow-through on commitments and for achieving outcomes.

What needs improvement?

An effective teacher leader sets the resolution of a pressing concern as a goal, gathers data to support the need for change, engages like-minded colleagues, and secures resources to make changes. Keeping the vision of a better world for students, teacher leaders persist to find ways to achieve their goals. Tichy warned us that "vision without execution equals hallucination" (Harris, 2003, ¶ 6). So teacher leaders move beyond vision, take action, and are responsible for the outcomes.

Persistence is the key to their success. With limited formal power, even in a formal role, teacher leaders know that they have to rely on their personal power to influence others, and they rarely let go of the desire to achieve desired outcomes. Ferren (2000) suggested that it takes "random acts of responsibility" committed each day to be a leader (¶ 1). Teacher leaders may achieve only partial success, but they recognize that "half a loaf" is an incremental step and may lead to an ultimate solution (Barth, 2007, p. 25).

In a study of effective professional learning communities, teachers reported that one of the most important types of support the principal provided was consistent follow-through on decisions (Moller et al., 2000). If this is true for principals, then it also applies to teacher leadership. Trust is built through experience with how much you can depend on another person. Follow-through on leadership responsibilities is important for ensuring that the principal and other teachers have trust in a teacher leader. As we have discussed teacher leadership with principals, we have found that one of the primary reasons for hesitating to share leadership is that these principals experienced disappointment when teachers became excited about a project, made a commitment to take the lead, and then did not follow through. Not only are teacher leaders accountable, but they also hold the same expectations for their colleagues.

TRUST

This definition of teacher leadership helps teachers to think differently about leadership and encourages teachers to consider leadership in their schools. In contrast to an authoritarian model of leadership, this definition more closely parallels what many teachers do already. It gives them confidence to acknowledge that they are or can be leaders and still maintain their relationships with their peers.

With this definition in mind, we share descriptions of three potential teacher leaders. Each teacher faces challenges to stepping up to a leadership role.

Three Potential Teacher Leaders

Descriptions of three potential teacher leaders illustrate the promise of rousing the giant of teacher leadership. Most educators will recognize these situations as typical.

Latonya

An elementary teacher for five years, Latonya experienced what she believed to be an excellent preservice preparation program at a nearby university. She entered the profession with knowledge of content, instructional strategies, and communication skills that help her interact effectively with students, parents, and her peers. Latonya works with experienced teachers in a school that is governed by a school leadership team that includes teachers, parents, and administrators as well as several local community members. Latonya plans and teaches with a team of fourth grade teachers whose students meet with success. She mentors preservice teachers from the nearby university on a regular basis. Her principal recognizes her competence and often recommends her to serve on committees in the school district. She has visited other schools to observe innovations. She is encouraged by the feedback she gets from parents on her work with their children. Often she visits families in their homes when parents find it difficult to attend parent-teacher conferences.

Currently, Latonya wrestles with the role she takes in the school's change efforts. She worries about how other teachers perceive her. Do they suspect that she is hoping to move into administration, even though her real motivation is to improve daily life at school for her students and her colleagues? Latonya wonders how other teachers will react if she offers to facilitate a study group so that teachers can share ideas and materials from the professional reading they are doing. Sometimes Latonya thinks she is too assertive in meetings and wonders if she may offend her colleagues by proposing too many changes. Last week she feared she was intimidating other teachers on the school improvement team. How much leadership she should exert is a concern for Latonya.

George

Recognizing the unlimited possibilities of teacher leadership would also be helpful for George, a music teacher who works in an urban high school. Two years ago, George left his vocation of performing with a band to become a teacher. A dedicated and competent professional teacher, George is pleased he made the switch but experiences frustration with the lack of change in the traditional high school where he teaches. George meets obstacles when he tries to persuade others that his music program should be expanded further to meet student needs. When he joined the school advisory committee, he found that little was accomplished. His experience in working outside the school in the community would, he thinks, really help facilitate the work of this committee.

After two years as a classroom teacher, he decided to pursue a master's degree. George would also like to share and to apply knowledge he is gaining in his graduate courses to the problems faced in his high school. Test scores at his school could be improved; student drop-out rates are alarming. There is much improvement needed in his school. He feels that, except within the fine arts department, his colleagues will neither listen to his thinking nor value his expertise. He hesitates to step forward, though he thinks he has something to contribute. George ponders whether his principal and his colleagues will be supportive of his leadership on schoolwide issues.

Miranda

Miranda is a special education teacher in a middle school. Over 20 years ago, she started teaching with most of the same teachers in this school. Two new middle schools opened recently in the district, and attendance boundaries changed. Her school's student population also changed drastically. Rather than the middle-class suburban population that Miranda and her colleagues have worked with for years, they are now teaching students from neighborhoods where poverty, unstable family structures, and substance abuse are prevalent. The students do not respond well to the curriculum and instructional strategies of the past. Miranda knows that the demands of a diverse student population require change in her school. She feels alone in this belief. She wants to help her colleagues cope with the new challenges they face rather than join them in doing things the way they have always done them. She recently was awarded certification from the National Board for

Professional Teaching Standards and has gained confidence in her ability as a teacher leader.

Miranda would like to lead discussions with her colleagues to invite them to solve instructional problems they face. Possibly she will talk to her principal about trying to find time for professional development activities targeted to middle school strategies. She would like to initiate some coteaching inclusion strategies with a regular education colleague. She believes these approaches can help teachers cope with the changes in their student population. She feels ready to step out and exercise her leadership, but she wonders how much impact she will have on reluctant teachers who seem to value maintaining the status quo.

Dilemmas similar to those of Latonya, George, and Miranda are not unusual. These teachers can play an even broader leadership role in the improvement of teaching and learning in their schools. However, administrators, other teachers, and, most important, the structures of schools may not support the contributions such teachers could make. Not seeing teacher leadership as a legitimate activity supported by others may keep teachers like these from contributing in significant ways to change in their schools.

We view the roles available to teachers like Latonya, George, and Miranda broadly. The sheer number of possible roles for teacher leaders in schools and districts lends credence to the idea that there truly is a huge untapped resource in schools. Surprisingly, though, may of these teachers do not see themselves as leaders unless opportunities are provided for them to reflect on their potential to lead.

Readiness for Teacher Leadership

Teachers benefit from conversations designed to raise their awareness about teacher leadership. This discussion is prerequisite to teachers thinking about their development as teacher leaders. In school systems, district staff members often ask us to help principals identify teacher leaders. How do we know who is a teacher leader or has the potential to be a teacher leader? It is easy to identify the formal teacher leaders, because they have titles and assigned responsibilities. The informal leaders are the teachers who practice their craft in subtle ways that may not be obvious to others. We use three adjectives to help teachers and administrators identify potential teacher leaders: *competent, credible,* and *approachable.* Teachers usually know which teachers are competent within their classrooms, and this naturally establishes them as credible. Being approachable is a critical characteristic. There are some teachers who are competent and credible but who choose to work as individuals rather than in collaboration with others. The ability to build positive relationships is critical to becoming a teacher leader.

A valuable conversation can be initiated by raising an individual teacher's awareness about his or her potential for leadership or about recognition of fellow colleagues as potential leaders. Am I a teacher leader? Do I have the potential to be a teacher leader? What characteristics do teachers need to have to become leaders? Which of my fellow teachers might also be identified as leaders? If answering these questions helps teachers more fully understand teacher leadership, then they may be ready to explore their own development as leaders and support the development of their colleagues.

One strategy to begin exploring teacher leadership is to use the instrument in Figure 1.1. This is an instrument to measure readiness for teacher leadership. Once teachers are open to considering that it is their responsibility to be leaders, the checklist is a tool to generate conversation around the concept. We use this instrument as we work with groups of teachers who are relatively unfamiliar with the idea of teacher leadership. It is useful for groups of preservice teachers or experienced teachers.

Who Is Responsible?

The responsibility for the development of teacher leaders is not limited to a single individual or group. Too often, the entire obligation is placed on the shoulders of the school principal. Others share in this responsibility. Teachers, superintendents, and district administrators, as well as leaders in colleges and universities, can be excellent advocates for teacher leadership.

Teachers

Teachers are responsible for the support of teacher leadership. The giant cannot be awakened without teacher leaders inviting others to join together in a community of leaders. By establishing collaborative relationships among faculty members, teachers begin to take the first step toward establishing an environment in which teacher leadership can thrive. The social relationships of teachers within a school are powerful determiners of how teachers assuming leadership roles will be viewed. Members of powerful cliques within a school can encourage or inhibit teachers who are willing to take on leadership roles.

Figure 1.1 Teacher Leadership Readiness Instrument

Assessing Your Readiness for

Teacher Leadership

Respond to the following statements in terms of how strongly you agree or disagree	Strongly Disagree	Disagree	No Opinion	Agree	Strongly Agree
1. My work as a teacher is both meaningful and important.					✓ (circled)
2. Individual teachers should be able to influence how other teachers think about, plan for, and conduct their work with students.				✓	✓ (circled)
3. Teachers should be recognized for trying new teaching strategies whether they succeed or fail.					✓ (circled)
4. Teachers should decide on the best methods of meeting educational goals set by policymaking groups (e.g., school boards, state departments of education).					✓ (circled)
5. I am willing to observe and provide feedback to fellow teachers.				✓	✓ (circled)
6. I would like to spend time discussing my values and beliefs about teaching with my colleagues.				✓	✓ (circled)
7. It is important to me to have the respect of the administrators and other teachers at my school.					✓ (circled)

Respond to the following statements in terms of how strongly you agree or disagree	Strongly Disagree	Disagree	No Opinion	Agree	Strongly Agree
8. I would be willing to help a colleague who was having difficulty with his or her teaching.					✓
9. I can see the points of view of my colleagues, parents, and students.				✓	
10. I would give my time to help select new faculty members for my school.					✓
11. I try to work as a facilitator of the work of students in my classroom and of colleagues in meetings at my school.					✓
12. Teachers working collaboratively should be able to influence practice in their schools.					✓
13. I can continue to serve as a classroom teacher and become a leader in my school.				✓	
14. Cooperating with my colleagues is more important than competing with them.					✓
15. I would give my time to help plan professional development activities at my school.					✓
16. My work contributes to the overall success of our school program.					✓

(Continued)

Figure 1.1 (Continued)

Respond to the following statements in terms of how strongly you agree or disagree	Strongly Disagree	Disagree	No Opinion	Agree	Strongly Agree
17. Mentoring new teachers is part of my responsibility as a professional teacher.					✓
18. School faculty and university faculty can mutually benefit from working together.					✓
19. I would be willing to give my time to participate in making decisions about such things as instructional materials, allocation of resources, student assignments, and organization of the school day.					✓
20. I value time spent working with my colleagues on curriculum and instructional matters.					✓
21. I am very effective in working with almost all of my colleagues.					✓
22. I have knowledge, information, and skills that can help students be successful.				✓	✗
23. I recognize and value points of view that are different from mine.				✓	✓
24. I am very effective in working with almost all of my students.					✓
25. I want to work in an environment where I am recognized and valued as a professional.					✓

Assessing Your Readiness for Teacher Leadership
Scoring Protocol

1. Count the number of times you chose "strongly disagree."
   Multiply by minus two (–2), and write the number here: _____

2. Count the number of times you chose "disagree."
   Multiply by minus one (–1), and write the number here: _____

3. Ignore the number of times you chose "no opinion."

4. Count the number of times you chose "agree."
   Write the number here: _____

5. Count the number of times you chose "strongly agree."
   Multiply by two (2), and write the number here: _____

6. **Write the sum of these four numbers here:**

If the number on line 6 is between 35 and 50

> Virtually all of your attitudes, values, and
> beliefs parallel those related to teacher
> leadership.

If the number on line 6 is between 20 and 34

> The majority of your attitudes, values, and
> beliefs parallel those related to teacher
> leadership.

If the number on line 6 is between –5 and 19

> Some of your attitudes, values, and beliefs
> parallel those related to teacher
> leadership. Several do not.

If the number on line 6 is –6 or below

> Few of your attitudes, values, and beliefs
> parallel those related to teacher
> leadership.

Source: © Professional Development Center, 2004.

School Administrators

Principals or assistant principals can encourage or discourage teacher initiative. These formal school-site leaders are critical to empowering teachers as leaders. They are the primary models for teacher leaders in the school and may effectively model leadership strategies and skills that teacher leaders can use. A principal's willingness to share power and to be a colearner with teacher leaders to improve classroom practice provides support for teacher leadership. Removing barriers, providing resources, and actively listening can be the most important tasks a principal does for teacher leaders.

Yes!

Superintendents and District Staff

The school rests within a larger organization, the school district. In a two-school district or a district with hundreds of schools, the decision makers at the district level influence the learning of the adults within the entire system. The influence can be tangible, such as resources allocated to professional development, or it can be intangible, such as setting the expectation that employees will learn. Just like in schools, where principals set the tone for change, superintendents and their staffs are responsible for providing the type of support that frees and encourages schools to prepare teachers as leaders. Superintendents and other staff in a school district can legitimize the efforts of developing teacher leadership by establishing appropriate policy and district culture and by being advocates for teacher leadership.

Colleges and Universities

The role of the colleges and universities in preparing teacher leaders is significant in the continuum of teacher development. The expectation that leadership is a teacher's responsibility can be cultivated early in the undergraduate preparation of the individual (Sherrill, 1999). Collaborative arrangements, such as professional development schools or learning consortia, connect teachers with university personnel. Standards and licensure for teacher leaders are being explored in many states, so professors are beginning to examine the content of their courses to assure they are preparing their graduates for leadership roles. Development of knowledge, skills, beliefs, and attitudes about teacher leadership begins with the university or college preparation programs for future teachers. Graduate programs and courses are emerging across the country

Like authentic shared

specifically designed to prepare practicing teachers for leadership. The leadership skills are as important in these programs as the curriculum and instruction content. After the teacher leaves the university, the goal should be to encourage that teacher to be a leader.

Conclusion

The giant resource of teacher leadership must be unleashed in the support of improved student learning. When teachers recognize that they can be leaders and accept a leading role from among the array of roles available to them, positive results in schools will follow. Teacher acceptance of leadership roles, appropriate professional development, and advocacy from formal leaders in the school system can start building a critical mass of teacher leaders to improve schools. The importance of teachers in complex, ongoing, educational change efforts cannot be overstated.

APPLICATION CHALLENGES

For Teachers

1. Help teacher colleagues to see the value of teacher leadership in improving student outcomes by opening the discussion in your school. Be positive, share your knowledge of the concept, and engage others in discussion. Emphasize the benefits to the improvement of teaching and learning for students, the retention of teachers, and the possibility to sustain change in the school setting. Work together to influence your principal's understanding of teacher leadership and its value.

2. Tap into the many resources available to develop yourself as a teacher leader (see Resource D). Professional reading, networking with other teacher leaders, and online communications can assist you in growing your understanding of teacher leadership and in building your own capacity.

For Principals

1. Build the confidence of teachers to be leaders. Make yourself available for regular interactions with prospective teacher leaders, and authentically listen to their ideas. Support teachers in initiatives

they wish to lead, and remove barriers to their success. Find ways to give incentives (e.g., release time, resources, recognition, and problem solving assistance) to teachers who are willing to take on leadership.

2. Grow professionally yourself in understanding teacher leadership and its possible impact on student outcomes in your building. Assure that you model professional learning and collaboration, and then work toward empowering the teachers rather than controlling them. Share professional readings and resources with teachers. Engage them in meaningful dialogue about teaching and learning.

For Superintendents and District-Level Administrators

1. Recognize that changes in schools are enhanced by a balance of efforts from the top down and the bottom up. Attempt to put policy and practice into place that pave the way for teacher leadership. Reflect on specific ways the school district can support teacher leaders, make resources available, and provide opportunities for networking.

2. Model leadership by working collaboratively with school administrators in ways that you would like to see principals and assistant principals work with teacher leaders. Create an understanding of teacher leadership among your building administrators, and encourage them to empower teachers in the same ways you empower your administrators.

For College and University Professors

1. Introduce the concept of teachers acting as leaders early in the preservice experience. Engage teacher education students in collaborative work, and build their skills to be fully functioning members of school cultures in which professional learning communities thrive. Emphasize the linkages between teacher collaboration and improved student outcomes.

2. Examine your curriculum and preparation programs for opportunities for preservice teachers to gain a broad perspective on formal and informal leadership opportunities for teachers. Assess the extent to which your programs are encouraging leadership rather than followership among your graduates.

2

Promoting
Teacher Leadership

*It is a new day for teachers! I believe the new leadership roles that
teachers are taking on in schools will allow us to serve children
better and will have a lasting impact on student achievement.*

Betsy Rogers, 2003 National Teacher of the Year

Struggling to understand why teachers should take on leadership
roles, advocating for shared power and responsibility, and
designing teacher leadership development programs has helped us to
clarify our own values and beliefs. Teacher leadership has the potential to influence significant school change and improved student outcomes, and both of these are fundamental reasons for expending
energy to promote it. Being able to articulate the *what* and *why* of
teacher leadership enables advocates to lead discussions that influence both reluctant teachers and decision makers to consider powerful models of teacher involvement.

Why bother to promote the idea of teacher leadership? What's
in it for all of us who are concerned about schools and student outcomes? To begin we examine the rationale for teacher leadership.
Teacher leadership can be viewed from four different, but related,

Purpose

23

perspectives. Each one provides support for promoting teacher leadership. Next, we share what we believe are the benefits of teacher leadership if it reaches its full potential. We end this chapter by sharing nine assumptions that serve as underpinnings for this book.

Rationale for Teacher Leadership

The *why* for promoting teacher leadership rests on a foundation of four perspectives, and each of these is a lens through which to view the purpose of building teacher leadership. There certainly are other perspectives, but we have found these to be the most helpful for us as we worked to develop teacher leadership. These perspectives are

Building organizational capacity.

Modeling democratic communities.

Empowering teachers.

Enhancing teacher professionalism.

Building Organizational Capacity

What we know about teaching and learning has taken quantum leaps during the early 21st century. Cognitive researchers are exposing us to knowledge that provides us with startling challenges to what we have in the past believed about *how* we learn and *who* can learn. Many educators are dismayed by the pressures generated by the No Child Left Behind legislation, but one of the clear benefits has been the focus on all students' learning. While this is an honorable goal, the reality is that many educators and others in our society were educated under systems in which some students were held to higher expectations because of who they were, while other students were expected to learn less or even fail. We do not have the luxury of these belief systems any longer, because all students must acquire high-level cognitive skills if they are going to function within an ever-changing world.

Today, the bar has been raised; expectations for all teachers and students are staggering. Resnick and Hall (1998) made a compelling argument for the significant professional learning necessary for teachers to move from an old theory of learning to a new theory. Table 2.1

Table 2.1 Moving From the Old Theories to the New Theories About Teaching and Learning

	Old Theory	*New Theory*
Learning	Build and strengthen bonds through practice and rewards	Construct own meaning by understanding own thinking using prior knowledge
Teaching	Break subject into sequential components Frequent testing Practice until learned Minimal connection among components	Systematic teaching to help students construct meaning and gain knowledge
Teacher	Manages externally produced programs	Asks questions and presents challenges to make students accountable to find solutions
Aptitude	Mostly hereditary Low expectations for some students, who are not taught a challenging curriculum	Effort and reflective problem solving to improve ability of all students

Source: Adapted from Resnick and Hall, 1998.

offers a comparative view of the old and new theories of teaching, learning, teachers' roles, and views of student aptitude. Attempts to break away from "drill and kill" approaches led to general agreement that students learn best through "knowledge-based constructivist" approaches, but these approaches bring with them broad implications for the professional learning of teachers. The constructivist model depends on teachers' deep knowledge of their subject area, of how to teach the subject, and of how students learn the subject (Sykes, 1999, p. 153), and these requirements place rigorous demands on teacher learning.

To address the increased need for teacher learning, effective professional developers adopt the model of professional learning communities, which provide a venue for teacher collaboration to aid in their learning. The reasons for promoting this model are numerous, but the most important is that schools must build their organizational capacity so their teachers can provide instruction of a type that they may never have experienced. Recognizing the sacredness of teacher autonomy is important, but somehow leaders must build a school culture in which teacher individualism is honored while insisting on a unified approach to student learning and quality professional learning for all teachers.

The key to effectively bringing a school together to collectively learn is building teacher leadership. Teachers are the people who can be counted on to remain through administrative turnovers in order to sustain initiatives to improve teacher and student learning. For this reason, collective learning within a professional learning community is not a fad but is rather the only reasonable approach to building and sustaining organizational capacity.

Modeling Democratic Communities

When we wrote the first edition of this book in the 1990s, the educational community was scrambling to find models for restructuring. Because the pressure to improve education was coming primarily from the private sector, the inclination was to look at business models for school reform. Schools trying to improve their product—student achievement—employed quality teams, strategic plans, and other business management strategies. Too often, well-designed business models were translated into mechanical approaches that teachers rejected, because the methods used too much of their time, and they saw little benefit for their students.

Educators' disillusionment with the business management approaches led to a return to the philosophical roots of schooling—democracy. Many educators recognized that the complexity of teaching is best addressed within a democratic community that responds to the uniqueness of the school context. In addition, when teachers take on leadership roles beyond the classroom, their schools can become democratic, and the more democratic a school culture, "the more students come to believe in, practice, and sustain our democratic form of governance" (Institute for Educational Leadership, 2001, p. 10). This shared leadership reflects the tenets of democracy by relying on the talents of all members of the school community, but with the increased accountability today, democracy has been sidelined in many schools.

Building a democratic community requires courage on the part of both principals and teachers, because the work is difficult. There are at least four challenges that educators face in creating a democratic model. First, leadership is ubiquitous in many organizations; principals, teachers, and other staff take on leadership roles based on their expertise, interests, and personal needs. A desired outcome of this leadership is that teachers, or others, who are recognized as having a solution to common concerns are asked to share their expertise so that everyone can benefit from their success. An obstacle to meeting this goal can be the school's culture. Is sharing practice accepted or rejected by colleagues? Are there teacher leaders who put their personal needs ahead of the students' needs? Rather than passing around leadership opportunities, does the school rely on the knowledge and skills of a few teachers who may or may not be positive teacher leaders?

Second, school administrators may be unwilling to share power through democratic decision making. During their graduate programs, potential administrators learn about the pitfalls they may face related to school law, personnel litigation, and budgeting challenges, and they may begin to fear the risks of sharing leadership. Or their willingness to share leadership may be impacted by the little leeway in school-site decision making they are given from the central office leaders. Although we would hope that all principals would be willing to involve teachers and share decisions in spite of the tough legal and fiscal responsibilities they have, in fact, a national survey indicates that "teachers, of all groups surveyed, feel the most ignored, with 70 percent saying they are left out of the decision making process" (Farkas, Foley, & Duffet, 2001, p. 3).

Third, teachers and principals may describe their school as a family in order to show how they participate in a community. The congeniality, whether real or contrived, is comfortable and, at the same time, can be debilitating. The metaphor of a family preserves the hierarchical structure in which the administrators are the parents and the other faculty and staff members are dependent children (Hargreaves & Fullan, 1998). A democratic community, on the other hand, assumes that all participants are equal and contribute value through their participation.

Finally, there is another dilemma for leaders in democratic communities. Conflict may result when members of the democratic community disagree on important matters and do not possess effective means of resolving their differences. Confronting actions by teachers that violate the school's vision is daunting and may divide the faculty. For example, tracking students into different-level classes may be promoted as an efficient strategy for the teachers, but it might contradict the school's vision of equity, and when teachers who want to track students are confronted by the members of the community upholding their school's vision, conflict will most likely occur. Rather than fostering self-interest, if our schools are to be democratic communities, they must model the type of collaboration so necessary for democracy with the inclusion of empowered teachers.

Empowering Teachers

Organizational development and leadership theory suggest that the active involvement of individuals at all levels in an organization is necessary to implement and sustain change. Over 20 years ago, recognizing that teachers are the closest to the clients, reformers acknowledged that unless teachers were involved in the decision making around the innovation, there was little chance that the reform efforts would succeed. Similarly, Maeroff (1988), then a senior fellow at Carnegie Foundation for the Advancement of Teaching, described a survey conducted by his organization that revealed how teachers felt about their involvement in decision making. The teachers reported they were substantively involved in only two dimensions of classroom and school policy—choosing textbooks and instructional materials and shaping the curriculum. In eight other areas, the teachers did not feel involved:

Setting standards for student behavior

Deciding whether students are tracked into special classes

Designing staff development and in-service programs

Setting promotion and retention policies

Deciding school budgets

Evaluating teacher performance

Selecting new teachers

Selecting new administrators (Maeroff, 1988, p. 56)

Today, these areas are still relevant for teachers, and there are not enough schools where teachers are empowered to be involved in making decisions in all or even some of these areas. Ingersoll (2007), in his extensive research on power, control, and accountability in schools, found that

> schools in which teachers have more control over key school-wide and classroom decisions have fewer problems with student misbehavior, show more collegiality and cooperation

Yes!

among teachers and administrators, have a more committed and engaged teaching staff, and do a better job of retaining their teachers. (p. 24)

Schools struggle to build meaningful teacher–administrator partnerships that result in powerful decisions for students. Principals who are successful discover that empowering teachers does not mean a loss of power for themselves but actually increases their power within the organization. Principals who share with us about their work with teacher leaders also reveal how surprised they are that their own stress level has been reduced, because they are not the only adults in the school shouldering the responsibilities. There are principals we have encountered who have had the courage to put aside their power to veto legitimate leadership team decisions. This level of collaboration is not easy at first, because it requires the principal to build the capacity of others to take on these tasks, but the outcomes usually outweigh this initial investment.

When power is shared, leadership is no longer defined within a person; rather it is an attribute that moves from person to person within the workplace depending on the situation and who holds the power. Can you lead without power? Do only formal leaders have power? The concept of power is uncomfortable for many teachers, who may feel the word *power* has negative connotations. It is true that power can be used either positively or negatively. Hersey and Natemeyer (1979) described two types of power—positional and personal. A person receives positional power by holding formal authority, such as filling a specific job role or a position appointed by the central office. In contrast, personal power is the result of the actions of the individual. Table 2.2 offers an overview of these power bases. Leaders at all levels of the school community use these power bases. Teachers primarily rely on the personal power bases in their relationships with other adults. The ability to influence others relies on teacher leaders' interpersonal relationships, their competence as perceived by others, and the information they have that others want to know.

Enhancing Teacher Professionalism

Every classroom must be led by a professional teacher. In order to achieve this goal, attention must be paid to the identification, development, and continued support of these valued educators. One of the benchmarks for determining professionalism is the individual's ability to control her or his work. Hirsch and Emerick (2006), representing

Table 2.2   Power Bases

Positional Power	*Personal Power*
Reward power is based on the perceived power to determine distributions of rewards. When a teacher wants to attend a national conference, it is often the principal who approves this request as a reward.	*Referent power* is based on identification with the leader. Teachers may identify with a principal who frequently teaches a class, understands curriculum, and monitors student progress, because they may perceive the principal to be more like them.
Legitimate power is based on the perceived authority to prescribe behavior. The principal in the school is designated by the school board as having the right to exert power in the school.	*Expert power* is based on the perception of the leader's special knowledge or expertise. A competent teacher is able to influence others, because this teacher has credibility within the school.
Connection power is based on the perception that the leader has relationships with influential people inside or outside the school organization. A superintendent of schools is usually perceived as having connection power within the system and outside the system.	

Source: Adapted from Hersey and Natemeyer, 1979.

the Center for Teaching Quality, reported that in five states where the Teacher Working Conditions Survey was administered, teachers reported that "if they are given sufficient time and control over what they do, their students will learn" (p. 13).

With the multitude of mandates placed on teachers in this age of accountability, few teachers report that they feel like professionals. Rather than honoring the intelligence and abilities of teachers as professionals, the efforts to ensure that all students learn have led to more control, directives, and stress; further, these changes result in many teachers feeling powerless, and in too many cases, teachers are leaving the profession. Teachers know what a professional teacher knows and can do. Ask faculty members to identify professional teachers in their school, and without hesitation, they can. Sockett found that teachers identified professionalism as competence in the following areas: "(1) character, (2) commitment to change and continuous improvement, (3) subject knowledge, (4) pedagogical knowledge, and (5) obligations and working relationships beyond the classroom" (as cited in Tichenor & Tichenor, 2005, p. 92).

Schön (1987), in his seminal work with reflective practitioners, found that professionals do not work from bureaucratic rules and regulations but instead work from principles and create their own guidelines for practice. The justification policymakers cite for mandating programs that control teachers' work is that a well-designed instructional package is better than the instruction delivered by a poor teacher. Although we recognize that good implementation of a packaged program may be better than ineffective teaching, we doubt that an incompetent teacher consistently uses a research-based program as the designers intended. A better approach is to enlist teacher leaders within a school to support teachers who are not succeeding in their teaching.

Although both the number of teacher leaders and the variety of teacher leader roles are increasing, still most teachers do not perceive themselves as professionals, because they are working in the confines of a classroom, which limits their understanding of the larger educational community. Ingersoll and Smith (2003), when studying teacher turnover, concluded that 40% to 50% of new teachers leave the profession in the first five years. Why would they stay in this profession where they are isolated, not treated professionally, and have limited contact with other adults? When we ask teacher leaders and administrators who are working outside the classroom to indicate their willingness to return to the classroom, few people are willing. Their reluctance to move back into a classroom is related not only to the limited financial benefits of teaching; it is also related to the isolation and limited opportunities they experienced as classroom teachers.

Benefits of Teacher Leadership

Central to the discussion of teacher leadership are the myriad advantages to be gained from tapping into this rich resource. While much remains to be done in terms of large-scale quantitative studies to establish clear relationships between teacher leadership and its impact on student learning, there is much cause for hope in the findings of studies focused on teacher leadership that have been completed in the past two decades. We describe below several of the benefits that affect students, parents, schools, teacher colleagues, and, most important, the teacher leaders themselves.

Professional Efficacy

When teachers see themselves as leaders, they discover the potential to influence student learning through their own actions. This is the reason most of us became educators in the first place—to make a difference with our students. Teachers who are successful with students and believe they make a difference exhibit professional efficacy. This sense of efficacy encourages teachers to move the locus of control for student results to themselves and to place less blame on factors beyond their control, such as the students' home environments. Linking teacher leadership to efficacy in their classrooms can help teachers understand how they can touch the lives of more students.

Retain Excellent Teachers

Teacher isolation, the absence of career ladders, low salaries, and the lack of leadership opportunities contribute to teacher attrition. It is generally recognized that there is not a teacher shortage; instead, we are not retaining quality teachers, and this is a "costly problem that is spiraling out of control" (National Commission for Teaching and America's Future, 2007, p. 4). Restructuring the school as a workplace for teacher leaders to have collaborative interactions is one initiative that can lead to more satisfaction with the work conditions and can encourage talented teachers to remain in the profession. Teacher leadership opportunities can promote teaching as a more desirable career and help to retain outstanding teachers for the complex tasks of school change.

Overcome Resistance to Change

Teachers who stay in education become discouraged with the multiple innovations imposed by those outside the classroom and by mandates that make instruction routine. Failure to include teachers in leading the implementation of innovations results in resistance to change. Credible teacher leaders can influence their colleagues to examine options and make decisions to try new practices. When teacher leaders participate in shaping and leading the change, there is

Positives of teacher leaders →

less resistance. If teachers know another teacher has had success with a new approach, and the approach matches their own beliefs about what is best for students, they are more likely to adopt the innovation. This ripple effect of change throughout the school results from the influence of teacher leaders.

Career Enhancement

Changes touted as part of school reform efforts often focus on ineffective teachers. Perhaps a greater problem is how to provide an environment in which good teachers are motivated throughout their careers. Teacher leadership offers opportunities for adults in the school to expand their areas of influence. Teachers can discover ways to advance their careers horizontally, rather than up the traditional career ladder into school administration. Teachers can be revitalized through the challenge of leadership roles.

Improve Own Performance

People learn what they teach. In a leadership role, teachers can improve their own instructional skills by helping other practitioners (Ovando, 1994). Working as staff developers, peer coaches, and curriculum specialists provides teachers with opportunities to examine their own practices while helping others to learn. This type of work encourages reflection among all participants. Teachers who complete the certification process through the National Board for Professional Teaching Standards report significant learning through reflection on their teaching practice. Teacher leaders learn through classroom observations and coaching, faculty study groups, and conducting action research within their own and others' classrooms.

Influence Other Teachers

As schools are presently organized, the principal influences the climate of the school, but this person can only touch the lives of a limited number of people. G. Donaldson (2006) suggests that principals must disavow themselves of the notion that they can be leaders to everyone in the school. Teacher leaders can collaborate with principals who are overwhelmed with demands from both within and outside the school. This offers teachers opportunities to encourage other teachers as well as to influence practices and policies in their schools. Holding the respect of their colleagues, capable teacher leaders can mentor new teachers, assist in improving instructional practice, and help to develop the capacity of other teachers.

Pros of Teacher Leaders

Accountability for Results

As authority for making decisions moves closer to those who must carry out the decisions, teachers become more accountable for their students' learning. Given the pressures of high-stakes testing, principals, out of a sense of responsibility, often hold onto the decision making power. A collective responsibility for student achievement could help the principal let go and move toward shared leadership and accountability. Teachers will be reluctant to take responsibility for results over which they have little control. As teachers are given authority to make student-related curriculum and instructional decisions, they will better understand how they are responsible for student outcomes. The ultimate value of teacher leadership is improved practice and increased student performance. Principals and teachers together can accept collective responsibility for these results.

Sustainability

Innovations in schools take time to be introduced and used proficiently. Regardless of the scope of the change, time is the critical element to ensuring that teachers and others in the school effectively use the innovation. To rely on one leader in the school to maintain the momentum for innovation is risky, because school systems transfer principals, key teachers retire or leave the system, and those remaining at the school are left to keep change moving forward. While we know strong instructional leadership makes a difference to outcomes, longitudinal studies also tell us that when strong instructional leaders exit a school, the improvement agenda is often slowed, halted, or in the worst cases reversed (Hargreaves & Fink, 2004). A critical mass of teacher leaders can make a difference by taking responsibility for moving forward while the new leadership is established in the school.

Teacher Leadership Assumptions

As we developed our definition of teacher leadership (see Chapter 1), we talked about the assumptions that influence what we believe about teacher leadership. These assumptions evolved as we were impacted by our discussions with teacher leaders and other colleagues, who feel passionately about these ideas.

We encourage others to engage in discussion within professional communities about these assumptions to better understand teacher leadership. Although these ideas are more complex than the "either/or" statements we present here, the juxtaposition of the two alternative assumptions stimulates conversation.

Assumption #1: All Teachers Versus Selected Teachers

These are two entirely different assumptions about the inclusion of teachers in leadership roles. Some people consider teacher leadership roles to be for a selected few, whereas others see empowered and professional roles for more teachers. Many principals pride themselves on including teachers in meaningful ways, such as in decision making or delivery of professional development. In reality, these leadership roles may be offered only to a few individuals, who are called upon repeatedly. Inclusion of only a few teachers in leadership roles can send a negative message to others. The teachers in appointed leadership roles are the professional teachers, whereas the rest of the teachers are technicians who carry out the decisions made by others.

As we define teacher leadership, our emphasis is on engaging all teachers in leadership activities to reach the goal of building a community of teacher leaders in each school. To develop the leadership of every teacher, it is necessary to build relationships and identify the niche where each person's skill, talent, or passion can be tapped.

Assumption #2: Either Formal or Informal Leadership Versus Both Formal and Informal Leadership

Informal leadership emerges based on the teacher's interest and the perceived needs of the school. In contrast, a formal teacher leader role is defined by a job description, sanctioned by district and school site administration, and built into the organizational structure of the school. Both types of teacher leadership may be critical to a well-functioning school.

There are people who believe that teacher leadership should simply emerge within a powerful professional learning community. This type of informal leadership is reliant on a healthy school culture, a competent teaching staff, and the willingness of the teachers to work together. Although this model should be a goal of every school, there are relatively few schools that have achieved it. Realistically, with time constraints, variations in teacher competence, and changing student populations, most schools must rely on both formal and informal teacher leadership. Rather than limiting the options for teacher leaders, the needs of the schools and their students should determine the forms of leadership undertaken.

Assumption #3: Classroom-Based Versus Administration-Based Leadership

A difficult decision for teachers who want to work with other teachers is whether or not to leave the classroom. Our belief is that teacher leaders can stay in their classrooms if they choose. They can still take the opportunity to exert broad influence both with students in their classrooms and throughout the school community. Many schools build structures to enable teachers to serve as leaders outside the classroom and still influence teaching and learning. For example, teachers may teach students part of the day and spend the remainder of the time coaching other teachers in their classrooms.

Appealing to teachers' interest in their students as a significant component of teacher leadership is more effective with most teachers than suggesting they take authoritarian positions that place them in roles as supervisors of their peers. Conversations about how teacher leadership has a different focus than administrative leadership invites teachers to see themselves as contributing to their colleagues' and students' success rather than separating themselves from their colleagues and students. The creation of a large number of roles, such as those of reading and math coaches, has challenged teacher leaders to walk the line between these two ways of viewing their leadership and to learn ways of influencing their peers without the positional authority that administrative positions provide.

Assumption #4: Primary Focus on Teaching and Learning Versus Primary Focus on Organizational Issues

Many teachers find that their involvement in schoolwide change is not satisfying. Frustrated with the disparity between the time they spend on schoolwide issues and the return on their investment in terms of their students, these professionals become disillusioned. The ongoing meetings and discussions may not center on the day-to-day lives of their students. Site-based governance structures, meant to bring about school change, at times become bogged down in issues, and not enough attention is paid to students' needs.

Teacher leaders are not limited to governance activities as the only route to influencing teaching and learning. By taking on roles such as teacher of a demonstration classroom, peer coach, action researcher, and study group leader, teachers have the potential to influence teaching and learning. This is where many teacher leaders want to focus their attention and are most willing to invest their time and energy; teacher leaders want to engage in work that benefits their students directly.

Assumption #5: Responsibility for Outcomes Versus Powerlessness

A parallel responsibility with shared leadership is shared accountability. Teacher leaders accept both the opportunities and the responsibilities that come with leadership. Just as the people with the closest affiliation with teaching and learning are accountable for student outcomes, teacher leaders are accountable for their responsibilities. Simply opening leadership roles for teachers may not make a difference in improving student performance. Only when teachers have both the chance to be involved and the accountability for progress will teacher-led change be meaningful. Then, teachers' efforts result in their solving authentic problems, and they can measure the outcomes of their leadership efforts with concrete evidence of school improvement and positive impact on student outcomes.

Assumption #6: Leaders Are Born Versus Leadership Can Be Learned

The concept of a born leader is an illusion. Although effective interpersonal skills and high levels of initiative may be considered prerequisites for a person being selected for a leadership role, leadership skills can be learned. The abundance of leadership courses, books on how to lead, and journals devoted to the study of leadership attest to the potential for learning leadership skills. Few superintendents would hire a principal or curriculum supervisor without graduate work in educational leadership. We believe that teacher leaders are shortchanged when we assume they can take on leadership roles without effective professional development. Teacher leaders must be given opportunities to practice and apply what they learn about leadership. Their school and district leaders must also be committed to encouraging and coaching teacher leaders' application of leadership knowledge and skills.

Assumption #7: Results-Driven Quality Professional Development Versus Disconnected Staff Development Workshops

Professional development for teacher leaders requires a substantial commitment. In contrast to participating in scattered workshops designed to introduce teaching strategies, we suggest that teacher leaders benefit from collaborating within and beyond their own schools, examining their assumptions about teaching and learning, and reflecting on their own practice. To enhance the development of teacher leaders, it is critical to take a planned, purposeful, systematic approach to professional development rather than provide haphazard and fragmented episodic initiatives. Long-term professional development for teacher leaders requires multiple forms of job-embedded learning, follow-up to ensure transfer, and application in the school context as well as ongoing participation in a learning community with colleagues both in and beyond their schools (Hawley & Valli, 1999). Teacher leadership requires moving beyond the notion that teachers can easily move from theories taught in graduate courses and in-service workshops to applying theories in the classroom; teacher leadership requires teachers to solve the multifaceted problems that they encounter daily in classrooms and schools and to create knowledge themselves that is willingly shared with colleagues.

Assumption #8: Reflective Teacher as Professional Versus Teacher as Technician

Policy mandates, decisions made without teacher representation, demanding school district supervisors, or principals who control school decisions demean the professional role of teacher leaders. When the emphasis is placed on student learning and outcomes, teachers can no longer be viewed as technicians who master a certain set of skills or techniques (Lieberman & Miller, 1999). Rather, teachers should be engaged in the intellectual work of continuous learning through inquiry and reflection. Teachers who are leaders see themselves as researchers, scholars, and problem solvers for improving student learning. These are roles not of technicians but of professionals who use their skills to address the unique problems of their schools. Teachers enter the profession with the expectation that they will have the autonomy to be creative in their work with students. Given today's emphasis on academic standards and accountability, these teachers are challenged and motivated by the notion that they will have responsibility for designing the instruction to help students meet the standards. Sadly, within a short time after beginning their teaching careers, many teachers realize that they do not have autonomy, as they are faced with many mandates that inhibit their ability to determine their own work.

Professional teachers need autonomy to meet the unique needs of their students. As well-meaning and knowledgeable as people outside the classroom might be, they do not work with the students on a day-to-day basis, nor do they have direct knowledge of how each student responds to the instruction. Surely the failed efforts of many school reform efforts over the past two decades should have taught us that teachers do not improve practice by being mandated to follow prescribed directives or to use "teacherproof" materials.

These assumptions are the driving themes that influence our definition of teacher leadership and that are reflected throughout the remainder of the book.

Conclusion

Teacher leadership is far from pervasive in our nation's schools. Since the early 1990s when we began our work with teacher leadership, more research has been completed, dissertations have been written, and books and articles on teacher leadership have increased, but there is still much more effort needed to promote, support, and sustain teacher leadership. The rationale for teacher leadership rests on the foundations of building organizational capacity, modeling democratic communities, empowering teachers, and enhancing teacher professionalism. The benefits of teacher leadership are becoming more publicly known, and we have noted those that we and others have observed, such as teacher efficacy, sustainability of change, and retention of teachers. There is, however, work still to be done to verify through research the linkages between teacher leadership and student outcomes. Just as we have formulated our thinking about the value of teacher leadership, we believe others will benefit from considering deeply their own and others' assumptions about the concept. Through this process, we have come to believe that when schools embrace the potential of teacher leadership, then teachers, administrators, and students all will reap benefits.

APPLICATION CHALLENGES

For Teachers

1. Form a study group at your school for interested persons who want to discuss the value of teacher leadership. Invite participants to begin with reading and reacting to the assumptions related to teacher leadership we shared in this chapter.

2. Parents may be allies in advancing the cause of teacher leadership in your school and district. Seek opportunities to share your beliefs about teacher leadership and the benefits it may have on student outcomes. Enlist the support of parents in influencing policymakers.

For Principals and Assistant Principals

1. To what extent have you created a professional democratic community in your school? Think about the ways you might encourage teachers' involvement and contributions. Develop strategies to engage teachers more fully in decision making at your site.

2. Reflect on ways in which you are building organizational capacity in your school. How do we use data to enable teachers to meet the needs of all of their students so that all students are given the time and opportunity to learn?

For Superintendents and District Staff

1. Reflect on the retention rate for teachers in your district. Teacher isolation, the lack of career ladders, and lack of teacher involvement are all reasons for the high attrition rates in our profession. Spend time in schools, observe teacher working conditions, and then think about how your district can positively make changes to impact teachers' work lives, by providing intrinsic rewards and opportunities for growth and development.

2. Discuss among your district staff personnel the potential benefits of teacher leadership for your schools and students. Examine how your work as district leaders can promote both the promise and reality of teachers engaged in leadership in your schools. Engage your school-site leaders in similar discussions, and then create a plan for promoting teacher leadership in your district.

For College and University Professors

1. Discuss how your institution might engage teacher leaders from surrounding school districts to teach undergraduate courses, mentor your undergraduate students, or serve on committees with your faculty. Study the impact of their involvement on them as leaders as well as on the quality of the programs offered to undergraduates.

2. Develop a collaborative research agenda with school district partners that engages them in measuring the impact of teacher leaders in their schools and districts and the linkages between teacher leadership and student outcomes.

3

Developing
Teacher Leaders

It might be hard to conceive how a group of worn-out teachers in comfortable shoes and paste-encrusted denim jumpers could gather in a school library at 3:35 and—without so much as fresh coffee, let alone a $1000/day professional trainer—solve real problems in education. But they can, and do.

Nancy Flanagan, Music Teacher Leader

Over the last 20 years, we learned most about teacher leadership by being involved with the professional development of teachers themselves. Almost 15 years ago, as we sat outside on the lawn of a university in South Florida, we shared our frustrations with the leadership development work we were doing with school-based and district administrators, including the lack of impact we were having. During that conversation, the idea that we were missing a significant group with potential for leadership was born; members of this group were teachers. We asked ourselves what we could do about it and determined that the contribution we could make would be in creating ways to develop leadership among teachers. And so began our work with teacher leadership.

As a result, our focus on professional learning moved to include potential teacher leaders. While we know that effective professional development is key to enabling all teachers and, in particular, teacher leaders to meet their full potential, years after our initial efforts began, there is still much to be done. School reform and improving student outcomes in our nation's schools is clearly linked to the emergence of a critical mass of teachers who, with leadership knowledge and skills, can influence other teachers to learn and improve their practice. These efforts cannot be the traditional professional development of the past, in which teachers were gathered into a room for a three-hour in-service session; rather these efforts must reflect quality professional development that is relevant and rigorous. Snell and Swanson (2000) commented, "If [we] hope to develop the critical mass of teachers who will be needed to reach challenging goals, an important place to start will be to provide all teachers with more opportunities to participate in rigorous, content-rich, collegial professional development" (p. 20). Like all educators, these teacher leaders deserve quality professional learning experiences. Teacher leadership and teacher learning are closely linked. Teacher leaders can develop the knowledge, skills, and attitudes that will allow them first to successfully work with their own students. Then, as continuing learners who model effective practice, they can impact colleague teachers and lead other teachers in reform efforts within their schools and school districts.

We cannot ask teachers to assume leadership roles without any preparation or coaching, simply because they appear to intuitively know how to work with their colleagues. Patterson (1993) warned us that "one of the worst forms of empowerment occurs when we turn people loose to implement tomorrow's organizational values without the necessary training to be effective in the new environment" (p. 62). Too often, we assume that *competent, credible,* and *approachable* teachers, who have instructional proficiency with their own students, are ready to be leaders; this assumes they should know how to work with other adults, understand the change process in schools, and grasp the potential challenges of their leadership work. When we look to individuals in other formal leadership positions, like principals or assistant principals, there is an expectation that these future administrators will be thoroughly prepared through meeting extensive educational requirements. Graduate programs for school administrators require numerous graduate courses. In many states, to be certified, applicants are required to pass competency tests and successfully complete an administrative internship in which candidates practice and get feedback on their leadership skills.

Rather than being provided extensive leadership preparation, teachers are asked to take on roles with their peers that could challenge the most gifted leader. Then, as evidenced by the frequent quick retreat from leadership roles (Little, 1996), teacher leaders run into complicated leadership issues that they feel they should know how to handle; when they cannot solve the problems, they blame themselves or others. The outcome is leadership burnout, and too often, they retreat from leadership opportunities to remain safe within the walls of their classrooms.

Because teacher leaders can make a difference in other teachers' learning and, therefore, student outcomes, their schools and school systems have a responsibility to prepare them to influence other stakeholders by providing them with leadership development throughout their careers. Development of teacher leaders must be viewed from a career-long perspective. The Southeast Center for Teaching Quality (2002) "recognizes a continuum of teacher growth and challenges participants to imagine larger roles for themselves as professionals" (p. 1). During preservice teacher education, a teacher leader's development begins with ensuring that the concept of teacher leadership is introduced, that opportunities for building self-awareness are offered, and that leadership skill building is part of the curriculum. These efforts lay the foundation for teacher leadership to develop during the induction and early years of a teacher's career and beyond.

In this chapter, we describe how these career-long learning opportunities to develop teachers as leaders could unfold. We begin by sharing what teacher leaders need to know about effective professional development for themselves and how guiding principles of professional development help them in working with other teachers' learning. Then, we propose ideas for preservice development of leadership potential among undergraduate students. Next, we share a self-assessment instrument that helps individuals determine how to grow as leaders; this can be used as teachers enter the profession and become aware of leadership opportunities. After that, we outline strategies and activities for continuous learning and support of the development of experienced teacher leaders throughout their careers. Finally, we propose a model for the development of teacher leaders that serves as a framework for all levels of leadership development.

Professional Development for Teacher Leaders

Much has been written and reported in the past decade about an idea that is at once both simple and complex. Simply stated, to improve American education, we must develop a highly qualified teacher workforce that will, in turn, use its knowledge, skills, and dispositions to ensure increasingly higher levels of performance of our K–12 students (Sykes, 1999). Building teachers' skills to achieve this goal is not an easy task; it involves complex approaches to increase their knowledge that will, in turn, alter their teaching. The key to meeting this challenge is enhancing the opportunities for teacher learning from the beginning to end of their careers. Teacher leaders are central to this goal; therefore, their leadership development is critical and requires investment throughout their careers.

Responsibility for Personal Leadership Development

Certainly, when teacher leaders engage with others in professional learning that includes studying data, planning collaboratively, improving instruction, and mentoring others, they are engaged in work that promotes their own learning while impacting the learning of others. When teachers learn and effectively use leadership skills such as communicating effectively, performing group leadership roles, or listening to identify thoughts and feelings of others, they are more successful in working collaboratively with their peers.

We would hope that school system leaders recognize their responsibilities for providing quality leadership development for teachers so that all teachers can develop individually and collectively, but this is not always the case. Teacher leaders should recognize and use their influence to assure that schools, districts, and universities are providing them with sufficient support. Recognizing quality professional development and making it a reality in schools is a challenge and one that teacher leaders can influence.

While it is beyond the scope of this book to provide a comprehensive description of what is known about quality professional development, there are numerous resources to help teacher leaders, and we have provided direction to find these resources (see Resource D). There are common principles that teacher leaders should know for their own and others' professional learning. For example, the Education Commission of the States (2000) suggested that learning needed to move beyond the simple transmission of knowledge and skills to teachers; it should engage teachers in authentic work that involves them in analysis, reflection, and problem solving on relevant issues to them, and ultimately empowers them to impact teaching and learning. Using the following questions as a guide, teacher leaders should ask themselves if the principles of effective design (Hawley & Valli, 1999) are honored in their own professional development.

Are adult learners, such as teacher leaders, involved in the identification of what they need to learn and in determining the process to be used for learning? This collaborative approach will likely result in increased motivation and commitment to learning.

Is school-based learning that allows for transfer and application of learning to immediate workplace problems provided in the work setting? This does not suggest that teacher leaders should not learn outside the school in teacher networks, graduate studies, or professional associations, because teachers do benefit from accessing knowledge and ideas outside the school. However, the motivation to learn increases and the impact on day-to-day practice increases with more learning experiences provided at the school site.

Are teacher leaders engaged in collaborative professional development? Collaborative strategies, such as action research and study groups, help solve real-world curriculum, instructional, and assessment problems teachers face.

Is professional development for teachers sustained and ongoing through follow-up coaching and support? Putting new knowledge into practice allows teachers to discover what works and does not and what additional needs they have for resources and assistance. Without access to ongoing support, there is a good chance teachers will abandon the strategies when they encounter difficulties.

The massive amount of learning necessary for teacher leaders to significantly influence schools of the future will require a new level of commitment from school and school system leaders and especially from the teacher leaders themselves. If the four requirements above are not being met, then teacher leaders must be prepared to advocate for change.

Responsibility for Others' Learning

Educators have long understood their responsibility for student learning; that is, they know the results for students are clearly impacted by their efforts as teachers. Lambert (2002) suggested that more recently educators have begun to recognize that they are responsible for their own learning as well and further that leadership is the professional work of everyone in the school. Teacher leaders who understand the challenge of learning and leading know that they must take personal responsibility for not only their own development but also the extent to which others in their schools have opportunities to develop. It is a collective endeavor. For many teachers, this is a new idea.

Teacher leaders who are committed to their own professional development recognize they must give a high priority to learning among the many responsibilities they have. These teacher leaders learn by reading professional literature and frequently take advantage of opportunities for higher education and professional networking within and outside the school. Feedback from colleagues is valued as a rich source of learning for these leaders; suggestions from others about how to be more effective are heeded, not ignored. Reflection on results in their classrooms and outcomes of their leadership activities allows these leaders to examine practice and learn from it. Often these teachers seek more challenging assignments or tasks so that they can learn from the experiences.

Similarly, teacher leaders take responsibility for the development of other teachers in the school setting. They may serve as facilitators or professional developers in their schools or districts. They may mentor new teachers or observe and coach teachers who are experiencing difficulties in their classrooms. The ideas, information, and resources shared by these teacher leaders empower others to be as effective as possible with students. These teacher leaders recognize the power of effectively modeling for other teachers and exhibit skillfulness in providing specific feedback so that colleagues can grow and develop.

Although teacher leadership has great potential for impacting school reform and student outcomes, we can approach it haphazardly or we can be prepared to provide teachers effective professional development that will enhance their leadership capacities. Our definition of teacher leadership implies that teachers have an obligation to participate together as learners and leaders. Our experience tells us they must be knowledgeable about effective developmental practices to influence development for themselves and others in the school and district. Accepting this responsibility and learning leadership skills does not happen quickly; it is a career-long commitment.

Leadership Development for Teachers

In order for teacher leadership to become an expectation in our profession, building a mind-set for leadership must begin during preservice education at the university level. As teachers enter schools, they are concerned with surviving within a new culture and with new students, but still these teachers can be encouraged from the beginning to see themselves as potential leaders. In addition, the idea of a being a teacher leader is new to many teachers, and they need entry leadership skills. As teachers become more secure in their leadership work, they may need a more complex set of professional learning experiences.

Preservice Teachers

If we are to expect that teachers will be able to step out of their classrooms to be leaders as a part of their daily activities, then we must engage in curriculum changes at the preservice level where teacher development begins. Troen and Boles (1994) placed responsibility on colleges of education for skill building among undergraduates: "Colleges of education must recognize the importance of teacher leadership and strengthen their commitment to teaching those skills as a required component of teacher education" (p. 279). Historically, undergraduate programs prepared teachers to be followers, not leaders, with an emphasis placed on supervising and controlling rather than encouraging personal accountability and empowerment. Among the strongest influencers on teachers' practice is the learning gained from their own experience as students in K–12 classrooms, what Lortie (1975) long ago called "apprenticeship of observation."

Today, preservice teachers must be asked to look outside their experiences to envision a better future for the profession and to accept responsibility for taking on leadership roles early in their preparation programs. An individualistic focus has been at the heart of preparing teachers for our nation's classrooms. Presently, to prepare teachers to learn effectively throughout their careers, we must move beyond individualism to ground their beliefs in a spirit of collegiality and to guide their practice toward working collaboratively with others. Helping preservice teachers understand the connection among professional learning, teacher leading, and student outcomes is of high priority. Preservice teachers must develop an understanding that working together with others in the interests of *all* students, not just *my* students, is "an integral part of their future work . . . and that leadership is not a privilege for a few—but a cluster of functions to be shared by all school stakeholders" (Du, 2007, p. 194). One way is to ensure that students are given opportunities to observe and participate in leadership activities—like school improvement team meetings, faculty advisory councils, or study groups led by teachers—during their school-site observations and practice teaching experiences. These firsthand experiences will enable them to open their minds to the potential of teacher leadership.

Undergraduate programs can also engage students in building self-awareness through the use of assessment instruments that provide prospective teachers with feedback on their communication and leadership styles. These data provide valuable insights for those who would be leaders in the future.

In addition, leadership skill building should begin at the preservice level. Prerequisite to working successfully in school cultures, where collective inquiry should be the norm, is developing skills in working effectively on teams, carrying out various roles in groups, and working together with others to solve classroom problems to improve instruction. Leadership skills to support this collaborative work include building relationships with others, leading small groups, developing teamwork, advocating a position by providing a rationale and using supporting data, and effectively managing conflicts. All of these efforts lay the foundation for teacher leadership to develop during the induction and early years of a teacher's career.

Potential Teacher Leaders

As teachers enter the profession, gain experience, and begin to move beyond survival, they gain expertise and, hopefully, begin to actually address students' unique instructional needs by utilizing assessment data to plan or modify instruction, and, with reflection, to alter their own teaching practices. Committed teachers who meet with success often begin to look beyond their own classrooms to determine how they might influence teaching and learning for children and adults on a broader scale.

In Chapter 1, we offered the Teacher Leader Readiness instrument as a tool for teachers to ascertain if they were ready to take on leadership responsibilities in their schools. Once teachers determine that they are ready to accept this challenge, then it is the teacher's responsibility to seek and the school system's responsibility to provide leadership development for them. Our assumption is that leaders are not born; they grow and develop in knowledge, skills, and attitudes that make them great leaders. Working alone and feeling that they should intuitively know how to lead are formidable obstacles for teacher leaders, but learning leadership skills with others can help overcome these obstacles.

To provide a framework for school systems to use in their efforts to provide professional development for teacher leaders, we reached out to teacher leaders, district staff, and a panel of experts to explore and articulate standards for teacher leadership with indicators to describe what teachers should know and be able to do as leaders. Out of this work we created an instrument, the Teacher Leadership Self-Assessment (TLSA) (Figure 3.1). Designed for teachers to use at an early stage of leadership development, the TLSA measures potential teacher leaders on six scales: (1) self-awareness, leading change; (2) communication; (3) diversity; (4) instructional proficiency; (5) continuous improvement; and (6) self-organization.

Use of the TLSA by teacher leaders offers a way for them to make judgments about the extent to which they currently meet the teacher leadership standards and to identify areas in which they may wish to develop new behaviors and skills. This process of reflection provides teachers with results on which to plan for their future professional learning.

Continuous Professional Learning for Experienced Teacher Leaders

Leadership development requires the same level of support as any quality professional development effort. The principles of such support are teachers' involvement in decisions about their own learning, job-embedded learning at the school site, collaborative learning with others, and follow-up support and coaching. As teacher leaders move into roles of influence in their schools, they are more likely to be successful impacting teaching and ultimately student outcomes only if continuous learning is provided. Just because a teacher appears to be an effective teacher leader does not mean that the teacher's opportunities for leadership development should be ignored. Learning to lead is a lifetime challenge.

Numerous strategies can be effective in providing continuous learning and support for the work of experienced teacher leaders. We offer only four examples: action research, certification by the National Board for Professional Teaching Standards, professional development schools, and professional networks. The common element among these strategies is that they are all examples of effective professional development practice. Teachers are engaged in initiating and planning these kinds of professional development, and the activities for the most part are job-embedded and are focused at the school site and on the relevant

Figure 3.1   Teacher Leadership Self-Assessment (TLSA)

Teacher Leadership Self-Assessment

Marilyn and Bill Katzenmeyer

Please respond in terms of how frequently each statement is descriptive of your professional behavior.

	Never	Rarely	Some-times	Often	Always
1. I reflect on what I do well and also how I can improve as a classroom teacher.	①	②	③	④	⑤
2. I understand how my strengths and needs for development will impact my new role as a leader in my school.	①	②	③	④	⑤
3. I am clear about what I believe about teaching and learning.	①	②	③	④	⑤
4. I act in ways that are congruent with my values and philosophy when dealing with students and colleagues.	①	②	③	④	⑤
5. I seek feedback on how I might improve in my work setting.	①	②	③	④	⑤
6. At work I behave in ways that are ethical and meet expectations for a high level of professional performance.	①	②	③	④	⑤
Enter the total of items 1–6 in the space to the right	Total Items 1–6 ___24___				
7. I invite colleagues to work toward accomplishment of the vision and mission of the school.	①	②	③	④	⑤
8. I lead others in accomplishing tasks.	①	②	③	④	⑤
9. I involve colleagues when planning for change.	①	②	③	④	⑤
10. I understand the importance of school and district culture to improving student outcomes.	①	②	③	④	⑤
11. I work toward improving the culture of the school.	①	②	③	④	⑤
12. I am willing to spend time and effort building a team to improve my school.	①	②	③	④	⑤
Enter the total of items 7–12 in the space to the right	Total Items 7–12 ___23___				
13. I listen carefully to others.	①	②	③	④	⑤
14. I adjust my presentations to my audience.	①	②	③	④	⑤
15. I seek perspectives of others and can reflect others' thoughts and feelings with accuracy.	①	②	③	④	⑤
16. When facilitating small groups I keep the group members on-task and on-time.	①	②	③	④	⑤

Teacher Leadership Self-Assessment, Page 2
Respond in terms of how frequently each statement is desciptive of your professional behavior.

	Never	Rarely	Some-times	Often	Always
17. When leading meetings I am able to get almost everyone to participate.	①	②	③	④	⑤
18. I use electronic technology effectively to communicate with individuals and groups.	①	②	③	④	⑤

Enter the total of items 13-18 in the space to the right.   Total Items 13–18 __2__ 28

	Never	Rarely	Some-times	Often	Always
19. I understand that different points of view may be based on an individual's culture, religion, race or socioeconomic status.	①	②	③	④	⑤
20. I respect values and beliefs that may be different from mine.	①	②	③	④	⑤
21. I enjoy working with diverse groups of colleagues at school.	①	②	③	④	⑤
22. I work effectively with non-educators and persons with special interests.	①	②	③	④	⑤
23. I make special efforts to understand the beliefs and values of others.	①	②	③	④	⑤
24. I am willing to share my beliefs even when they are different from the beliefs of others.	①	②	③	④	⑤

Enter the total of items 19-24 in the space to the right   Total Items 19–24 __25__ 26

	Never	Rarely	Some-times	Often	Always
25. I promote a positive environment in the classroom.	①	②	③	④	⑤
26. I use research-based instructional practices.	①	②	③	④	⑤
27. I persist to assure the success of all students.	①	②	③	④	⑤
28. I have a reputation for being competent in the classroom.	①	②	③	④	⑤
29. I am approachable and open to sharing with colleagues.	①	②	③	④	⑤
30. I act with integrity and fairness when working with students or adults.	①	②	③	④	⑤

Enter the total of items 25-30 in the space to the rights   Total Items 25–30 __25__ 30

	Never	Rarely	Some-times	Often	Always
31. I seek out all pertinent information from many sources before making a decision or taking action.	①	②	③	④	⑤
32. I set goals and monitor progress towards meeting them.	①	②	③	④	⑤

(Continued)

Figure 3.1 (Continued)

Teacher Leadership Self-Assessment, Page 3 Respond in terms of how frequently each statement is descriptive of your professional behavior.	Never	Rarely	Some-times	Often	Always
33. I analyze and use assessment information when planning.	①	②	③	④	⑤
34. I participate in professional development and learning.	①	②	③	④	⑤
35. I am proactive in identifying problems and working to solve them.	①	②	③	④	⑤
36. I work side-by-side with colleagues, parents and / or others to make improvements in the school or district.	①	②	③	④	⑤
Enter the total of items 31-36 in the space to the right	Total Items 31–36 ___18___				
37. I plan and schedule thoroughly so that I can accomplish tasks and goals.	①	②	③	④	⑤
38. I exhibit self-confidence when under stress or in difficult situations.	①	②	③	④	⑤
39. I work effectively as a team member.	①	②	③	④	⑤
40. I show initiative and exhibit the energy needed to follow through to get desired results.	①	②	③	④	⑤
41. I prioritize so that I can assure there is time for important tasks.	①	②	③	④	⑤
42. I create a satisfactory balance between professional and personal aspects of my life.	①	②	③	④	⑤
Enter the total of items 37-42 in the space to the right	Total Items 37–42 ___20___				

Teacher Leadership Self-Assessment
Scale Descriptions and Scoring Protocol

Scales of the Teacher Leadership Self-Assessment

Self-Awareness: Teacher has an accurate picture of self in terms of strengths, values, philosophy and behaviors.

Leading Change: Teacher uses effective strategies to facilitate positive change.

Communication: Teacher exhibits effective listening, oral communication, presentation skills and expression in written communication.

Diversity: Teacher demonstrates respect for and responds to differences in perspectives.

Instructional Proficiency and Leadership: Teacher possesses and uses professional knowledge and skills in providing the most effective learning opportunities for students and adults.

Continuous Improvement: Teacher demonstrates commitment to reaching higher standards and readiness to take action to improve.

Self-Organization: Teacher establishes course of action and implements plans to accomplish results.

Self Scoring Procedure

✓ **Self-Awareness:**
Enter Total of Items 1–6 26

✓ **Leading Change:**
Enter Total of Items 7–12 23

✓ **Communication:**
Enter Total of Items 13–18 28

✓ **Diversity:**
Enter Total of Items 19–24 30

✓ **Instructional Proficiency:**
Enter Total of Items 25–30 30

✓ **Continuous Improvement:**
Enter Total of 31–36 29

✓ **Self-Organization:**
Enter Total of 37–42 26

ldt_self_assessment_separates4.wpd

problems and issues that teachers face. In addition, these strategies offer collaborative work with other teachers and are long-term, frequently providing high levels of support for the teacher leaders who are involved. In Table 3.1, we offer examples of possible strategies to stimulate the thinking of those who would like to influence the continuous learning and support for development of teacher leaders.

Table 3.1   Strategies for Continuous Development of Teacher Leaders

Strategy	Purpose	Benefits	To Learn More
Action Research	Engages teacher leaders in disciplined inquiry conducted to inform and improve practice by using the results and other research	Involves teachers in inquiry and gaining professional expertise Taps the current research base to add to professional knowledge of teachers Changes the school context by offering an opportunity for collective work Creates opportunities to improve instruction and improve student learning Calls upon teacher leaders to use data to make decisions about effectiveness of their practices in the classroom Provides opportunities for leadership of research groups and projects	Calhoun, E. (2002). Action research for school Improvement. *Educational Leadership, 59*(6), 18–24. Caro-Bruce, C., Flessner, R., Klehr, M., & Zeichner, K. (2007). *Creating equitable classrooms through action research.* Thousand Oaks, CA: Corwin. Sagor, R. (2004) *The action research guidebook: A four-step process for educators and school teams.* Thousand Oaks, CA: Corwin.
Certification by the National Board for Professional Teaching Standards	Uses rigorous standards to assess and grant national certification through involving teachers in a process of	Engages teachers in a rigorous process to analyze and to strengthen classroom practice Enables teachers to demonstrate leadership of students in the classroom as	Contact Information: National Board for Professional Teaching Standards 1525 Wilson Boulevard Suite 500 Arlington, VA

Strategy	Purpose	Benefits	To Learn More
	intensive study, expert evaluation, self-assessment, and peer review	well as leadership in the school, community, or with parents Offers opportunities for peer collaboration and feedback	22209 http://www.nbpts.org
Professional Development Schools	Builds partnerships between universities or colleges and K–12 schools to focus on the preparation of new teachers, faculty professional development, inquiry directed toward improved practice, and improvement of student achievement	Involves teacher leaders in the redesign and improvement of preservice and inservice teacher education Engages teachers in inquiry, research, and reflection to examine practice and to expand knowledge base Provides opportunities for collaborative and innovative work for teacher leaders	Lanier, J., & Darling-Hammond, L. (2005). *Professional development schools: Schools for developing a profession.* New York: Teachers College Press Organizations: National Council for Accreditation of Teacher Education (NCATE), www.ncate.org National Association for Professional Development Schools, www.napds.org
Professional Networks	Formal or informal communities of practice for teacher discourse, reflection, and learning, which may focus on particular subject areas, teaching methods, or approaches to	Allows teacher leaders to participate in and sustain ongoing professional learning Builds professional knowledge through sharing among teacher leaders Offers a highly interactive and social opportunity for teacher leaders to grow and develop	McLaughlin, M., & Talbert, J. (2001). *Professional Communities and the Work of High School Teaching.* Chicago: University of Chicago Press. Lieberman, A., & Wood, D. R. (2003). *Inside the National Writing Project: Connecting network learning and classroom teaching*

Table 3.1 (Continued)

Strategy	Purpose	Benefits	To Learn More
	reform; may be face-to-face or virtual; local or national	Provides experience in leading groups and participating successfully with colleagues	New York: Teachers College Press. Organization: Teacher Leader Network www.teacherleaders.org

A Development Model for Teacher Leadership

To prepare teachers for leadership roles, we propose a development model, Leadership Development for Teachers (LDT) (Figure 3.2), that provides a framework for professional learning beyond competency in teaching skills. With this model, we advocate that teachers developing as leaders collaborate with their peers to understand first themselves,

Figure 3.2   Leadership Development for Teachers Model

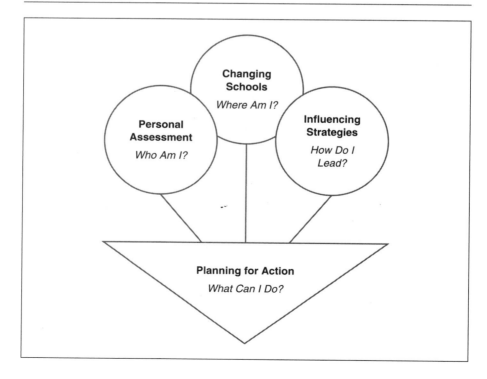

then their colleagues, and finally their schools. Ultimately, to fully acquire skills as teacher leaders, they must practice their skills in their work setting.

Three broad components of the model include *Personal Assessment, Changing Schools,* and *Influencing Strategies.* The final component, *Planning for Action,* engages participants in applying their newly developed leadership skills in their schools or school districts by carrying out an action learning project.

First, *Personal Assessment* invites teachers to examine their own beliefs. They answer the question, "Who am I?" in the educational context of their work. Personal assessment activities can help teachers recognize the values, behaviors, and philosophies that underlie their professional performance. Knowing their own perspectives leads to the recognition that their colleagues may be quite different and that successfully working together requires an acceptance of those differences. This alone can relieve the frustrations teacher leaders experience when they work with teachers who think or teach differently based on other assumptions. In addition, self-assessment provides an opportunity to reflect on the competencies and skills teachers bring to leadership roles. Teachers discover their own level of professional expertise and that of their colleagues in order to consider ways they might support or gain support from other teachers. Finally, knowledge of the various stages of adult development provides teacher leaders with a way to better understand themselves and the individuals within the school setting. In this way, teacher leaders may determine ways to best provide support to each individual. Once teachers gather data about themselves, they feel more comfortable seeking feedback to better understand how they are perceived by their colleagues.

Next, we believe teacher leaders benefit by understanding the *Changing School* in which they are trying to lead. Teachers sometimes bring only the perception of their classroom, their grade level, or their subject area to broader leadership roles. The question teacher leaders ought to consider is, "Where am I?" Teachers can benefit from reflecting on and analyzing their school cultures. We believe that teachers need to explore and create their own definition of teacher leadership and consider how teacher leadership is a necessary component of school improvement and change within the context of their school. Knowing what is supporting or hindering their leadership efforts within their setting provides insight and direction for their work as leaders. For example, whenever schools attempt to make change, conflict is a natural result. A thorough understanding of one's personal preferences in conflict situations and consideration of other behaviors aids teachers attempting to lead change to handle difficult situations. Teachers who have the big-picture perspective of the context within which they lead are better equipped to think more broadly about the whole school and about making change within that setting as well as within the larger context of the school district, the state, or national settings.

Third, teachers develop skills for *Influencing Others*. Asking the question, "How do I lead others?" shows recognition by teacher leaders that they can acquire a concrete set of strategies and skills to use in their daily roles. Recognizing that leading is not "knowing it all" or acting as an expert is valuable to teachers attempting to make positive changes in their schools. Learning to lead groups through the application of facilitative skills allows teacher leaders to hold effective meetings and accomplish work within their grade levels, teams, or the whole faculty. Teachers who would be leaders learn that to listen means more than hearing others. Skills in focusing on others, pausing to understand others' perspectives before sharing one's own, and looking for meaning beneath the words of others become valuable prerequisites to effective communication with colleagues. Another powerful set of skills for teacher leaders who want to successfully interact with others is recognizing how to deal with differences. Teacher leaders recognize that the skill set that can be applied in these situations includes acknowledging differences, disclosing one's own perspectives, and seeking to understand and use the perspectives of others.

Finally, the last component of the model, *Planning for Action*, engages teacher leaders in application-level learning; they must answer the question, "What can I do?" in their own schools. This interest in transferring and applying new knowledge, skills, and attitudes is an important piece of a development experience for teacher leaders. Beginning with recognition of what needs to change, planning includes gathering data related to the change, testing others' experience, and learning from the research; finally, setting goals and determining strategies for making the change is valuable to the teacher's growth. This is when teacher leaders put their skills into action. To learn new skills and not apply them within the school is nonproductive. Teacher leaders must make commitments to use their new leadership knowledge to improve their schools for all students. This is the purpose of teacher leadership. When teachers attempt to apply new leadership skills and knowledge in their classrooms and schools, the amount of support from the principal and other teachers will likely determine teacher leaders' success. Like other skills, leadership skills are fragile until the teacher leader practices them, gets feedback, and develops competence by using them.

The process of leadership development is not as linear as our model may suggest. Still, if teachers are offered the opportunity to tap into the vast leadership knowledge base, they will know that they are not alone in dealing with the frustrations of working with others. Leadership relies on building relationships and developing shared capacity to reach desired goals. It is as simple and as complex as that. In addition, teachers' participation in developing as teacher leaders results in improvements in self-confidence, teaching, and attitude toward work, and it expands teachers' knowledge and perspectives (O'Connor & Boles, 1992). Denying teacher leaders opportunities to learn leadership skills places their ability to lead at risk.

Conclusion

Career-long learning opportunities to develop teachers as leaders are needed if we are to adequately prepare teachers for leading the change in our nations' schools. Knowledge of effective professional development ensures both that teachers can demand the best learning experiences for themselves and that they will be able to assist with the development of others using effective methods. A career-long continuum of development for teachers leaders includes (1) preservice development of leadership potential among undergraduate students, (2) a self-assessment for use during the early years of teaching that identifies standards and indicators for entry-level teacher leaders and offers a strategy to help them plan their growth and development as teacher leaders, and (3) continuous learning and support of the development of experienced teacher leaders throughout their careers. The Leadership Development for Teachers model serves as a framework for all levels of leadership development. Professional development alone is not enough; the relationships, the context, and the skillful influencing of others are necessary for teacher leaders to make a significant difference.

Chapter 4 offers thoughts on the uniqueness of teacher leaders, generational differences among teacher leaders, and reluctant teacher leaders. Chapter 5 explores the school context necessary for teacher leadership to thrive, and Chapter 6 explicates the influencing skills and strategies that teacher leaders must apply to make a difference in teaching and student outcomes in their schools.

APPLICATION CHALLENGES

For Teachers

1. Learn more about effective professional development. Visit the National Staff Development Council's Web site at www.nsdc.org.

2. Explore the myriad professional development methods and strategies. Investigate and learn more about effective approaches to professional development such as Critical Friends' groups (see National School Reform Faculty, www.nsrfharmony.org/), mentoring, online learning, video reflections, induction programs, classroom walkthrough, study groups, professional learning communities, and collaborative planning.

For Principals

1. Consider how you will assure that your school's change initiatives will be continued if you leave or are transferred from your current school. How are you developing leadership among your teachers to maintain the focus over time on changes you worked with them to implement? How will you prepare teacher leaders for the inevitable time when you will be leaving the school?

2. Become an advocate for teacher leader preparation and development in your school and district. Consider how teacher leaders will be identified, engaged in planning for meaningful, long-term leadership development, and offered school-site opportunities to practice their skills. Think about how you will show that you value and reward teachers' efforts as they develop into leaders.

For Superintendents and District Staff

1. Assess your school district personnel practices and policies related to induction of new teachers, professional development for all faculty and staff, and performance appraisal. How can you move these practices and policies from traditional, hierarchical approaches toward those that are more collaborative in nature and capitalize on the leadership of teachers?

2. Examine how professional development for teachers is planned, delivered, and evaluated. Reflect with the district leaders and principals on how professional development can become more systematic, long-term, focused, and collaboratively planned with participants. How might you evaluate its effectiveness and cost-benefits?

For College and University Professors

1. Study your preservice teacher preparation program for areas in which the curriculum can be expanded to include teacher leadership awareness, leadership skill development, and observation by student interns of practicing teachers engaged in leadership.

2. Look into ways to engage university faculty in serving along with leaders in schools on action research teams, school leadership councils, or as mentors or coaches. Then think about how the university faculty members can glean from these experiences ways to improve teacher preparation programs and curriculum at the university level.

4

Understanding Myself and Others as Teachers and Leaders

Understanding strengths and weaknesses is the first step towards accepting one another—and towards maximizing the potential of collective action. Teams that overlook the personalities of their members end up frustrated and ineffective.

Bill Ferriter, Sixth Grade Teacher Leader

In working as colleagues over three decades on writing together and on various teacher leadership initiatives, we have come to know the strengths that each of us brings to the task. We have learned to capitalize on each of our unique strengths and shore up one another in our developmental areas. We learned early on to be honest with ourselves, because we recognized that whether we acknowledge our weaknesses or not, our colleagues still see them.

Similarly, this kind of self-awareness is critical to a teacher leader's success. As we work in developing teachers as leaders, many have shared with us that understanding themselves has led to their being much more effective in building relationships and in working effectively with others. In order to thrive as teacher leaders, they must recognize the factors that influence how they and their colleagues work, learn, and change in the workplace. Although the context influences teachers, their reactions to the context and consequent decisions to make behavioral changes happen internally. Hargreaves and Fullan (1996) said that "teaching is bound up in [teachers'] lives, biographies, with the kinds of people they have become" (p. 25). This uniqueness affects how they will approach their work and carry out leadership roles. Because of the importance of self-awareness for success in leadership roles, a major component in the development of teacher leaders is asking, "Who am I?" (Figure 4.1). Teacher leaders who pay attention to and learn from self-assessment information find that it is helpful both professionally and personally.

Before teachers presume to lead others, they should understand themselves. One of the scales on the Teacher Leader Self-Assessment instrument (see Chapter 3) measures a teacher leader's self-awareness. Items on the self-awareness scale of the assessment suggest that a teacher who is self-aware exhibits some of the following behaviors:

- Assesses own strengths and developmental needs as a teacher and a leader
- Recognizes own behaviors, values, and philosophy

Figure 4.1   Personal Assessment

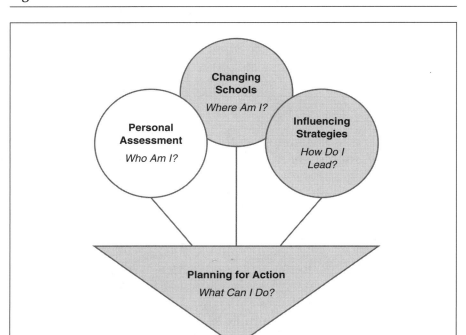

- Self-monitors own behavior for congruence with values and philosophy
- Seeks and uses feedback
- Reflects on practice and areas for improvement (Katzenmeyer & Katzenmeyer, 2004)

As teacher leaders grow and develop as individuals, they expand their spheres of influence by focusing attention on growth and development of not only themselves but also others in their schools through exhibiting the following behaviors:

Building relationships and trust with others

Inspiring and motivating others through feedback and providing opportunities to learn

Dealing with resistant or difficult colleagues

Entrusting others with responsibilities beyond regular job responsibilities

Modeling behaviors of a continuous learner

Acting as a mentor, coach, or counselor for colleagues (Katzenmeyer & Katzenmeyer, 2004)

When engaging in collaborative self-assessment activities, teachers soon recognize that their colleagues may have different sets of values, beliefs, concerns, philosophies, and behaviors. Rather than being frustrated with teachers who do not share their beliefs, teacher leaders can use skills to move beyond working with like-minded colleagues to engage a diverse group of teachers in a professional learning community. Teacher leaders' knowledge of differences and ability to value multiple perspectives help them use the strengths of these differences when leading individuals and groups.

Teacher Uniqueness

While educational change certainly occurs school by school, a more powerful change process occurs person to person. A faculty consists of people with differences in teaching skills, philosophies on how students learn, generational needs, work perspectives, willingness to interact with others, adult development levels, and personal lives (see Figure 4.2). In this chapter, we explore these

Figure 4.2   Factors Contributing to the Uniqueness of Teachers

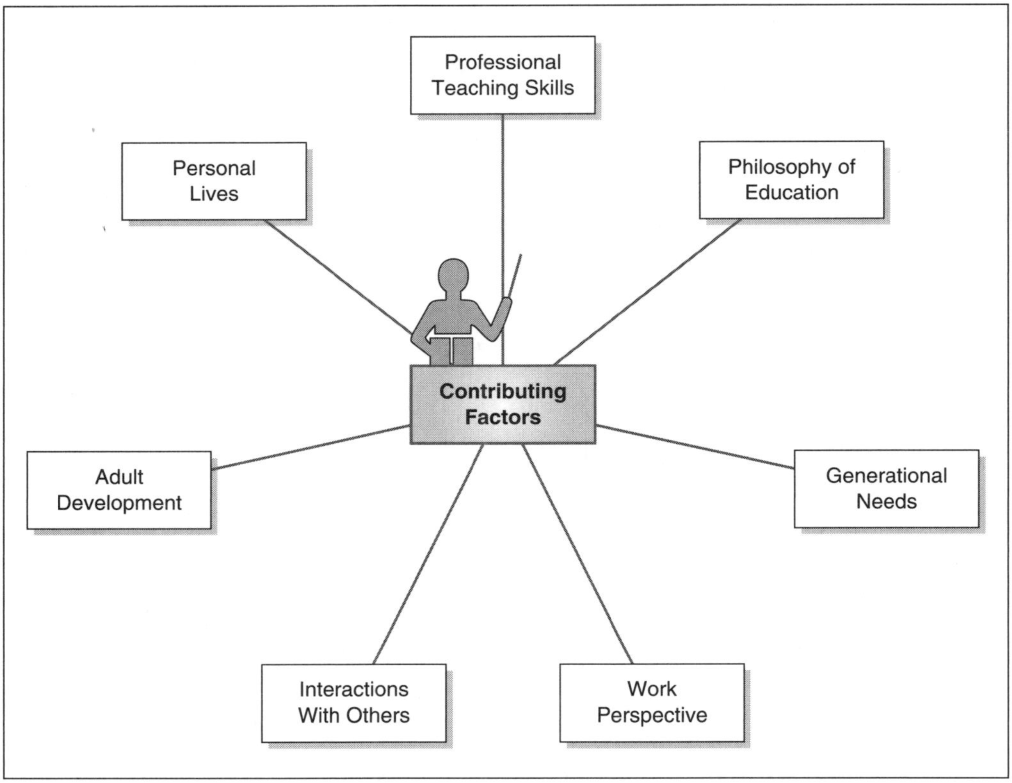

differences. Then we suggest that in order to work with a diverse group of teachers, we must each acknowledge and understand these differences in order to be more effective and experience less frustration.

Professional Teaching Skills

Before others will accept a teacher as a leader, that teacher must be successful with his or her students. Instructional proficiency is necessary to lead effectively with students in the classroom and to establish credibility with peers and administrators. The strategies may not be found in the lesson plans, but the teacher's ability to effectively adjust the instruction reflects a high level of skill development. If a teacher is not proficient in teaching skills, then the focus in the classroom is on a survival level. This teacher will need to develop classroom expertise before leading beyond the classroom. On the

Teacher Leader Self-Assessment, the scale that refers to these behaviors is called Instructional Proficiency and Leadership; that is, teacher leaders possess and use professional knowledge and skills in providing the most effective learning opportunities for both students and adults.

Teachers confident in their own abilities want to collaborate with colleagues. They are willing to explore new strategies and to expose their own insecurities about their teaching practice. Teachers who can be honest about their struggles in teaching are usually the ones who win the respect of their colleagues. Many teachers feel that they should know the answers—after all, they are teachers. Teaching, however, is an uncertain and complex craft (Cochran-Smith & Lytle, 2006), and when a respected teacher reveals uneasiness, it makes others feel they are not alone in feeling frustration.

One teacher described another teacher leader: "She has always been successful first with students. She always seems to know what she is doing and how to approach things in a quiet and supportive, dependable, enthusiastic way." As teachers become secure in their professional teaching skills, they are ready to reach out beyond the classroom to share with others. As one principal commented, "To me the highest accolade teachers can have is when their peers ask for help from them."

Personal Philosophy of Education

The current demands to gain a deeper knowledge of content, understand how to effectively teach the content, and recognize how students learn the content challenges teachers to confront what they believe about teaching and learning. Sykes (1999) suggested that "securing teachers' hearts and minds around organizational and curricular changes has been the Achilles heel of much reform" (p. 154). A teacher's personal philosophy of education can make this transition a challenge. For example, teachers' views of education may be based on their own experiences as young students. Teachers may remember success in their own schooling. It is difficult for them to think differently about schools when traditional education served them so well. School reform efforts may call into question teachers' assumptions about these past positive experiences. If they excelled as individuals competing for academic grades, then it may be difficult to embrace cooperative learning. These assumptions will influence the decisions teachers make and how they will lead others. Previously, we shared our assumptions (see Chapter 2) about teacher leadership; similarly, teachers bring a set of assumptions to their teaching. Rarely are teachers given opportunities to examine their own assumptions and then to compare them with their actual practice.

Little (1993) recommended that teacher leaders examine the underlying assumptions of school reform and compare the congruence of these underlying assumptions with their own existing beliefs, values, and practices. Inviting teachers to compare what they say they believe with their actions can also test their assumptions. For example, experienced teachers who say "beginning teachers should be supported" may find that their actions are incongruent with this belief. They may be reluctant to confront the practice of placing novice teachers with the most difficult classes in their school. We all experience discomfort when we realize that, although we say we believe one thing, it is evident that our actions are not consistent with our beliefs.

Teacher leaders may think that all teachers share their beliefs about discipline, homework, or other areas of concern. It is eye opening for teacher leaders to see how the views they assumed to be shared by all may be inconsistent with the views of their colleagues. Teachers are even more disturbed when they discover they do not share the predominant values of their schools. The focus of the school may be proclaimed through a lofty mission statement, but the actual practice in the school may violate the expressed mission and supporting values. Until this dissonance is resolved, teacher leaders may not be comfortable working toward common goals for the school. Some teachers leave schools to find other positions in different schools that have values congruent with what they believe.

A strategy we use to help teachers examine their belief systems about teaching and learning is requesting that they complete the Philosophy of Education Inventory (Zinn, 1996) found in Resource A. At first, the title of the instrument brings back memories of their teacher education programs, and teachers believe that they will be discussing "ivory tower" theory. After completing the instrument, the teachers compare scores with colleagues and discuss how they may prefer different teaching methods or hold different beliefs about their roles with students. Only then do teacher leaders begin to see the practical use of examining these underlying beliefs. They recognize differing philosophies of colleagues and see that the differences can cause conflict in decisions about curriculum, instructional practices, and assessment.

Generational Needs

Each generation is influenced by their past and the context in which they live. Similarly, teachers share needs similar to those of other members of their generation of professional colleagues. As the teachers from the baby boom generation (born 1946–1964) look toward retirement, there are two new groups of teachers entering the workforce, and these are people who have different needs and expectations for their careers. Teachers from Generation X (born 1965–1980) and Generation Y or Millennials (born 1981–1999) have differing values, beliefs, and perspectives on work and the workplace.

Today, few new teachers are committing to a lifelong career in education; most are exploring teaching or entering the profession from other careers. Table 4.1 shows the differences between the generations that present special challenges for cross-generational relationships within schools.

The balance between the needs of different generations is a major factor in today's schools. Baby boomer teachers often become frustrated when teachers from younger generations do not exhibit the same work ethic that boomers have held. On the other hand, younger teachers cannot see the value of jeopardizing their personal lives by spending inordinate amounts of time in the school workplace. Recent research, such as that conducted by the Project for the Next Generation of Teachers (www.gse.harvard.edu/~ngt/), suggests that current teacher leaders' idealism and willingness to work long hours, with few rewards, will not satisfy the new generation of teachers.

With the influx of teachers from other careers, the generational gap will continue in spite of the departure of the baby boomers. While individuals should not be stereotyped according to the characteristics of generational differences, teacher leaders can use this information as a guideline in relating to work groups and to teachers with a wide range of ages.

Work Perspectives

Teachers are influenced by their disposition toward a job. Staw's (1986) longitudinal study found that a person's disposition as a teenager can predict an attitude toward work in middle and late adulthood. A person's attitude toward his or her job seems to remain stable over the years (Schaubroeck, Ganster, & Kemmerer, 1996). Perhaps people are not as malleable as one would like to think they are. To change an attitude toward work requires strong interventions.

Table 4.1 Generational Expectations and Needs

*Baby Boomers (Born 1946–1964)	*Generation X (Born 1965–1980)	**Generation Y Millenials (Born 1981–1999)
• Thrive on hard work • Possess strong ideals • Put in long hours at personal expense • Became political to gain power • Demonstrate optimism and see everything as possible • Seek to make changes • Are competitive to separate themselves from the crowd • Expect a long-term career in one field or organization • Identify strongly with who they are in terms of what they do at work	• Demonstrate strong individualism; want to do things their way • Change jobs if needs are not met • Place high priority on quality of life • Want balance in life • Lack loyalty to specific career or organization • Desire flexibility • Exhibit technological savvy due to media that have sprung up during their lifetimes • Learned to be very resourceful due to violence and disruption in formative years • Demonstrate skepticism due to lack of permanence in families and institutions they have experienced • Act with self-reliance and do not rely on others or institutions	• See selves as multitasking champions • Are realistic, confident, and pragmatic • Prefer interactions via technology rather than face-to-face • Are naturally collaborative and want professional and social networks for learning • Are globally oriented • Are socially conscious • Want information shared and expect inclusion in decision making • Are used to plenty of positive feedback as have been coddled by parents; may be stunned by negative feedback • Expect diversity in the workplace; it is the norm for them • Expect structure, to work in teams, and to be part of the group • Exhibit self-confidence and want variety in their work

Sources: Items with * adapted from Carlson, 2004; Dittman, 2005; and Lancaster and Stillman, 2002. Items with ** adapted from Wong and Wong, 2007.

It often takes a critical incident to change a person's perspective. For example, a teacher's own child may experience difficulties in a traditional school environment, which stimulates that teacher to suddenly see the benefit of increased commitment to change in education.

Teachers' work perspectives affect how they balance their work with other parts of their lives. For instance, some teachers may view their responsibility to teaching as secondary to other life obligations. In contrast, other teachers may believe teaching is a mission and devote extra time and effort. Different perspectives on work can influence the leadership responsibilities these two groups of teachers may choose to accept. Teachers whose primary interests rest outside their work lives may want to provide leadership within the classroom and, perhaps, help a few colleagues. In contrast, teachers who feel a strong commitment to their profession may take on the leadership roles in groups within the school, which frequently require additional time beyond the regular workday. Those teachers who make large commitments toward school improvement are often impatient with teachers who do not. Teacher leaders must understand that not all teachers have the same level of interest in their work or life circumstances.

Interactions With Others

Teacher leadership demands frequent interactions with other adults. This may be uncomfortable for some teachers. One teacher leader told us, "During faculty discussions, I didn't hesitate to share. I was surprised that I took a risk—just the willingness to share and being open was a change for me." Interactions beyond the everyday conversations with others who work nearby force teacher leaders to deal with diverse ideas and speak out about their own beliefs.

Teachers working in collegial work environments are more effective, but within this collaboration, individual expression should be honored by acknowledging that some teachers may need time to work alone (Crowther, 2008). Teachers may prefer working by themselves for many reasons. As in the general population, there are those among teachers who are energized by contacts with others and those who are not. Teachers sometimes choose to work alone to conserve their most valuable resource, time.

On the other hand, there are teachers who would like to work together, yet the structure of the work environment does not encourage collaboration. These teachers want to be in the know about the happenings within the school. Sometimes these teachers want knowledge to lead positive change, but other times teachers may use this as an excuse to seek control that leads to negative consequences. One experienced teacher leader we know wanted to be deeply involved in all aspects of her school; she was impatient with teachers who chose not to be part of the decision making but then complained about the decisions being made. She believed that teacher leaders need to be a part of the solution, not part of the problem.

Selecting the best match between the desire to interact with others and a specific leadership role contributes to the success of a teacher. Those who prefer to work alone may be interested in roles such as developing grant proposals or writing curriculum materials. In contrast, the teacher who wants to interact with others may be more interested in coaching, speaking at community group meetings, or becoming a staff developer. As teachers examine their own needs, they will become clearer about the kinds of leadership activities that suit their individual styles.

Adult Development

Every day adults have opportunities to reflect and grow. Individuals can choose to develop, or they can continue to view the world from an existing perspective. More than 50 years of research from developmental psychology reveals that just as children have developmental needs, so do adults. Teachers' developmental stages influence their interactions with students, parents, and other staff members as well as their ability to lead others.

Leithwood (1992) developed a summary of the work of three developmental psychologists, resulting in a stage model that briefly describes adult growth. Table 4.2 provides descriptions adapted from his work.

Table 4.2   Adult Development Concerns

Stage 1: Self-Protective	**Stage 2: Conformist**
• Must obey rules, but tries to get own gain • Most questions have one answer • Fear of being caught • Blames others	• Needs approval in order to meet expectations of others • Feels guilty breaking rules • Tends to go along with the group and not accept individual differences
Stage 3: Conscientious	**Stage 4: Autonomous**
• Understands multiple possibilities • Recognizes there are exceptions to rules • Future oriented	• Fully independent • Understands the interdependence of relationships • Accepts others as they are

Source: Adapted from Leithwood, 1990.

The stages of development appear to be tidy categories, but adults are unpredictable and cannot be pigeonholed. Each of us is unique and exhibits behavior represented in different stages. Although other models exist, Leithwood's synthesis offers insight into teachers' stages of development. Teacher leaders who are at the *self-protective* stage may find open and honest communication to be uncomfortable. Teachers at the *conformist* stage tend to honor the status quo, finding it difficult to embrace change, unless other teachers with whom they identify want the change. Group decision making is a chore for these teachers, because they find different perspectives on issues annoying. In contrast, the teacher at the *conscientious* stage values consensus and would be effective as a facilitator or group member. At the *autonomous* stage, teachers not only see value in others' viewpoints but also draw strength from them as these teacher leaders take on schoolwide leadership responsibilities. As teachers move into higher levels of adult development, we find that they are less dependent on experts for solutions to problems. Instead, these teachers solve their own problems, often in collaboration with other colleagues. The more mature teachers will seek out experts only to fill in the gaps in their problem solving strategies.

Adult development and adult learning are complex. Drago-Severson (2004) recommended that school leaders purposefully plan for helping teachers to learn how to "better manage the complexities of work and life" (p. 17). This requires professional learning to move beyond learning knowledge, to helping teachers to make sense of what is happening to them and their students. In the process, teachers can gain not only in the technical skills of teaching but also in their own adult development.

Personal Lives

Although invitations to teacher leadership may be extended to all teachers, the reality of adult life is that teacher leadership may not be for all teachers throughout their careers. Acknowledging the transitions in the personal lives of teachers recognizes that there are times at which a teacher may be eager to participate, and there may be other times when the teacher may retreat from these responsibilities. For example, a mother of young children or an experienced teacher caring for elderly parents may need to relinquish leadership responsibilities in order to maintain balance in her life. As a teacher walks through the front door of a school, a whole person enters the community of teachers, administrators, students, and other staff members. It is impossible to completely compartmentalize personal and professional lives, because the "work self" exists in concert with other facets of a teacher's life, and attempts to isolate them are futile.

Teacher leaders put in long hours doing excellent work with their students and providing schoolwide leadership. Like other adults, teachers struggle with life issues. Problems with teenage children, family illness, marital difficulties, second jobs, community involvement, and other personal dilemmas occupy the minds of teachers as they shoulder leadership obligations. Often, concerns are expressed about students who live in difficult family situations, but teachers may experience similar types of problems in their own lives. Teachers' reluctance to take on leadership roles may stem not from a lack of interest but from a desire to protect the time they need to balance work and personal responsibilities. Teachers welcome options in their level of involvement in leadership responsibilities.

L. F. Zinn (1997) studied supports and barriers to teacher leadership. One area in which she found impeding factors was personal consideration and commitments. These are personal issues that a teacher may not share with other colleagues and that may lead to misunderstandings about why a teacher is not assuming leadership responsibilities. The factors in this area included

1. Family or other responsibilities that compete with leadership roles (e.g., crises, child-rearing, single parenthood, aging or infirm parents, illness of one or more family members).

2. Personal health issues or concerns.

3. Lack of family support for leadership efforts.

4. Cultural or religious values that discourage leadership. (p. 45)

The reality of teacher leaders' lives may compel them to move in and out of leadership roles. Dependence on a few teacher leaders in a school puts the school's reform efforts at risk. Because of these possible circumstances, the goal is to build the leadership capacity of all teachers in the school so that when a teacher leader must attend to personal issues, there are other teachers to assume the responsibilities.

Reluctant Learners and Leaders

In our work with teacher leaders, conversations often turn to complaints about other teachers who are perceived to be unenthusiastic about learning new instructional strategies or are unwilling to take on leadership roles when there is a need for more people to assume these roles. "If only . . ." statements are made about these reluctant learners and leaders. The factors described earlier in this chapter may account for many of the differences between a teacher with leadership initiative and a teacher who is unable or unwilling to make the commitment. Teacher leaders, according to G. Donaldson (2006), can best approach these situations by "recognizing the emotional and personal realities of their colleagues" (p. 131). Teacher leaders work to acknowledge the emotional realities found among their colleagues and to build caring relationships that honor the personal feelings and situations of their colleagues.

Disillusioned

Teachers may have begun their careers with an idealistic view, but after years of disappointment in frequently shifting innovations, they may protect themselves by refusing to accept change. Why should they become involved again? These are the teachers who become the cynics, yet they can be valuable resources during decision making about a new change effort. If encouraged, they may ask the difficult questions that may prevent a school from moving from one educational fad to another.

Keep the Status Quo

Teachers who feel they are secure in their teaching positions face three options. First, they can remain unchanged and teach as they have taught for years. Second, they can update their knowledge and skills to improve their performance in the classroom to meet today's challenges. Finally, these teachers may decide to move beyond the status quo to improve their professional skills and influence school change on a broader scale. Those teachers who want to remain stagnant in their instructional repertoire present a challenge to teacher leaders who are anxious to implement new ideas about teaching and learning.

Withdrawal

At any time, a teacher may withdraw from involvement. Interventions should occur early if they are to be successful with teachers who withdraw (Steffy, Wolfe, Pasch, & Enz, 1999). Unfortunately, the symptoms are hard to detect, because teachers who begin to withdraw become quiet and blend in with a compatible group of peers. Inviting teachers at this stage to accept even limited teacher leadership roles may be enough of an incentive to prevent them from moving into deeper levels of withdrawal.

Mediocrity

Few teachers come to their work to willingly teach poorly, but there are teachers who lack the necessary knowledge and skills to effectively teach students. When confronted, these teachers may blame the inability of their students to perform on external forces, such as poverty, family situations, and other factors. In the same school, though, there will most likely be teachers who are successfully working with the same or similar students. Faced with their deficits, these teachers usually become defensive, and directive supervisory approaches meet with little more that negligible compliance. Principals and teacher leaders can best encourage mediocre teachers by engaging them in meaningful collaborative experiences, such as joining a team of competent teachers visiting another school to observe best practices or coteaching with an effective colleague.

Incompetence

The incompetent teacher presents school leaders with a moral dilemma, because this is the person who violates professional ethics by causing harm to students, yet leaders may find that due process to remove this person from the profession can be demanding and politically charged, and little action may result beyond the school. Teacher leaders become incensed when they describe the incompetent teacher and often cannot understand how the school district leaders tolerate this behavior. Confronting an incompetent teacher is a primary responsibility of the formal leaders within the school and school system who hold the legitimate power to handle the issue.

Acknowledging Diversity

Being able to successfully collaborate with colleagues will require teacher leaders to understand how to work with others who are different from them. Because departmental, organizational, and academic divisions are highly segmented within schools, there are schools in which teachers seldom work with other teachers or may not even know the names of teachers in the same building. This is frequently true of large, impersonal secondary schools but may occur at all levels. Certainly the increasing student diversity within our schools and communities also suggests that these skills are of primary importance to teacher leaders. Teacher leaders who are skillful in dealing with diversity are aware of their own deeply held beliefs and values, and they work to understand the perspectives of others. A gifted teacher leader can bring together conflicting constituencies to make decisions and resolve issues.

We encourage teacher leaders to learn skills that will make them sensitive to seeing others' points of view. A first step may be to facilitate activities that focus teachers' attention on the diversity of educational philosophies in a specific school. Teacher leaders become alert to the various sets of beliefs and values that their colleagues, administrators, and parents bring to school. In our work, we find that the instrument Philosophy of Education Inventory (L. Zinn, 1996; see Resource A) helps teachers to measure their personal educational philosophy. Learning about the philosophies of others leads teachers to a deeper understanding of the different perspectives they encounter in making change happen at their schools. Teachers learn to effectively work with other people in their schools and in their communities by engaging in conversations with those who have different beliefs and experiences with education.

Teachers work with a broader group of stakeholders, including parents, students, and community representatives—all of whom bring their own perspectives to the school setting. In addition, teacher leaders work with others who come from diverse cultural and socioeconomic backgrounds. The neighborhood school in which everyone basically looked and thought the same no longer exists in most communities.

Learning skills to approach others who are different can enhance teacher leaders' abilities to work collaboratively with others. The ADS model (Figure 4.3) is designed to aid teacher leaders in using skillful communication in situations where differences exist. We suggest that teacher leaders learn to articulate and *acknowledge the differences* that exist, rather than ignoring them. For example, the English department and the social studies department may have different beliefs about grading. Or the community leader on the school improvement team may not share the views of a teacher in the group. Teacher leaders must learn to *disclose their values and views* by being open and honest with others. For example, a teacher might share with colleagues the progressive beliefs she holds about ways to work with students who have special needs. The teacher who holds a humanistic philosophy of education may disclose his views on the state testing program. Finally, teacher leaders should *seek to understand and include others.* Valuing individuals for the diversity they bring to the situation can be essential to the success of teacher leaders.

Figure 4.3   ADS Model

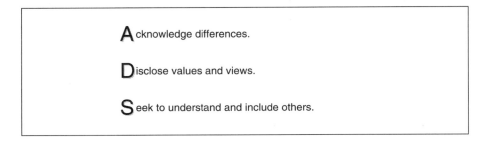

In our experience, teachers find it beneficial to enhance their abilities to use the ADS model in their work with others. Given the diverse environments in which teachers are trying to make change, these skills become valuable tools for teacher leaders to learn.

Conclusion

Experience with teacher leaders has taught us that personal assessment does not stop with understanding about one's self, important as those insights may be. The meaningful learning for these teachers has been in how they view their colleagues and their relationships with these colleagues. They recognize and acknowledge the differences that exist among their colleagues, and they learn that diversity is to be valued. We not only emphasize the importance of acknowledging these differences but also invite teacher leaders to reveal their own assumptions to encourage a deeper understanding of others.

Teacher leaders can look at their own assessments and predict how others may be the same or different; they can then use this information to be more effective in working with others. The insights help teacher leaders to know themselves better. Often they conclude that leadership involves changing one's own behavior to be productive with diverse individuals or groups. By acknowledging others' perspectives, teacher leaders honor the uniqueness among their colleagues.

Attention to the organizational environment in which teachers work is also necessary. If the school workplace does not reflect a rich learning climate for both students and staff, teacher leadership will not flourish. Teachers seek positions in schools that support the individual differences discussed in this chapter. If the goal is to improve all schools, then all schools need to provide healthy workplaces for adult growth and development. In Chapter 5, we discuss school cultures that support teacher leadership.

APPLICATION CHALLENGES

For Teachers

1. Develop greater understanding of yourself and your leadership work. Use a variety of approaches; for example, keep a journal on your experiences and reflect on the behaviors you exhibited and the results you gained. Or seek helpful feedback on your leadership of others from your principal or other trusted administrator with whom you work closely as well as from your peers and colleagues.

2. Identify a teacher at your school site who is reluctant to join in change efforts to improve teaching and learning. Use the Factors Relating to the Uniqueness of Teacher Leaders (Figure 4.2) to reflect on this teacher. Consider what factors might influence the individual's readiness or willingness to become involved. What might you do to rekindle the passion of this teacher and engage him or her in continuous improvement efforts in the school?

For Principals

1. Map your faculty according to the generational differences that might be present among your teachers. Consider strategies you might use to bridge the divide among your faculty members and to create a culture in which both new and experienced teachers collaborate regularly and benefit from the differing perspectives they bring.

2. Match the unique needs at your school with the individual teachers who have potential for leadership. Think about those teachers on staff who may have skills and talents that you have yet to discover. Encourage teachers to discuss with you their perspectives on a niche they might fill to improve teaching and learning. Work to develop your understanding of capabilities for leadership among your staff members. Avoid calling upon the same teachers repeatedly, and strive to discover new potential for leadership among your staff members.

For Superintendents and District Staff

1. Build the capacity of principals to understand teacher leadership and its potential. Consider engaging principals in writing a role description for teacher leaders, soliciting their input to district plans for supporting teacher leadership, or engaging them

in discussion about how teacher leadership is working at individual school sites.

2. Consider using district resources for offering ongoing professional development for teachers who wish to be formal or informal leaders in their schools. Assure that the professional development is effectively designed and delivered includes opportunities to practice leadership on the job, to gain valuable feedback from coaches or mentors, and to be supported with time, resources, and encouragement.

For College or University Professors

1. Include personal assessment opportunities in teacher preparation programs and coursework. Encourage preservice teachers to gain information about their communication styles, personality traits, and leadership styles. Encourage your students to maintain a portfolio of assessment information about themselves that can be continued as they are inducted into the profession.

2. Work collaboratively with school districts to understand the needs and challenges they face in filling teacher vacancies. Form partnerships and work together to produce teachers who see themselves as leaders of change and improvement in schools.

5

Building a Culture That Supports Teacher Leadership

Getting teachers and their instructional leaders (principals) on the same page about working conditions is more than just a good idea—it is a necessary step for genuine and sustained improvement in the quality of education for the majority of America's children.

Renee Moore, High School English Teacher Leader

One of the most important factors in supporting the development of teachers as leaders is the context of the school. Although individual teachers' dispositions, belief systems, and skills affect their ability to lead, the context of the school is central to their success. When competent teacher leaders become discouraged in their profession, the cause may well be the organization in which they work rather than their classroom experiences. Teacher attrition is not solely the result of the way teachers are prepared but also the result of the school environment that teachers encounter that causes teachers to experience alienation. These feelings of isolation, powerlessness, and meaninglessness explain the vast numbers of teachers leaving the profession, regardless of whether they are trained as teachers in traditional university or alternative programs.

Culture, according to Peterson and Deal (1998), is "the underground stream of norms, values, beliefs, traditions, and rituals that has built up over time as people work together, solve problems, and confront challenges" (p. 28). A positive culture within a school fosters teacher leadership, which in turn produces positive results in student outcomes (Anderson, 1992). As early as the mid-1990s, research findings confirmed that student achievement increases substantially in schools with collaborative work cultures (Newmann & Wehlage, 1995). Today, more emphasis is placed on creating professional learning communities within schools in order to provide a culture that is supportive of both student and faculty learning.

In our teacher leadership model, the "Where am I?" (Figure 5.1) places the emphasis on the context in which teachers attempt to exercise their leadership. Teacher leaders cannot influence others and put plans into action if the school context is not supportive of those initiatives.

Figure 5.1 School Context

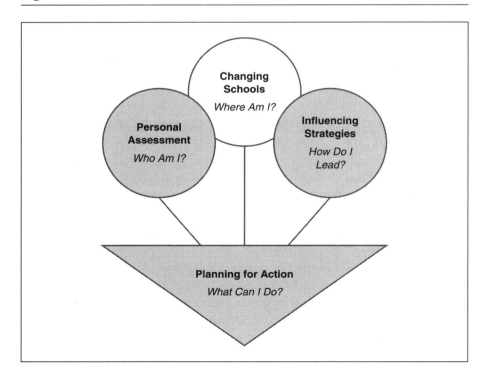

In this chapter we delve into the importance of school culture and the impact of context on the work of teacher leaders in improving schools and outcomes for their students. We offer a set of dimensions that we have found to be evident in schools in which teacher leadership thrives. Through sharing responses to interview questions asked of two aspiring teacher leaders, we provide examples of how the dimensions might be evidenced within schools that support or inhibit the practice of teacher leadership. Next we consider the importance of three factors in providing a context that supports teacher leadership: (1) the relationships between adults in the school, (2) the organizational structures, and (3) the actions of the principal.

Dimensions of School Culture

Our experiences in working within higher education have afforded us opportunities to engage with preservice teacher education students, both those who are traditionally aged and older, seasoned career-changers who bring their experiences in other organizations to their forthcoming teaching positions. We have marveled at the energy and enthusiasm of individuals from both groups who look forward to making a difference with students and who aspire to be teacher leaders in their schools. As we work with preservice teachers, we encourage them to analyze carefully the school context in which they choose to accept a teaching position and to consider their potential to become teacher leaders in that school.

To help them determine a healthy school culture for their leadership, we offer dimensions to guide their decision making. These dimensions of teacher leadership (Katzenmeyer & Katzenmeyer, 2005) include the following:

> *Developmental Focus:* Teachers are supported in learning new knowledge and skills and are encouraged to help others learn. They are provided with needed assistance, guidance, and coaching.

> *Recognition:* Teachers are respected and recognized for the professional roles they take and the contributions they make. A spirit of mutual respect and caring exists among teachers. There are processes to recognize effective work.

> *Autonomy:* Teachers are encouraged to take initiative in making improvements and innovations. Barriers are removed, and resources are found to support teachers' efforts.

Collegiality: Teachers collaborate on instructional and student-related matters. Examples of collegial behavior include teachers' discussing strategies, sharing materials, or observing in one another's classrooms.

Participation: Teachers are actively involved in making decisions and have input on important matters. Department or team leaders are selected with the participation of teachers.

Open Communication: Teachers send and receive communication in open, honest ways in the school. Teachers feel informed about what is going on in the school. Teachers easily share opinions and feelings. Teachers are not blamed when things go wrong.

Positive Environment: Teachers experience general satisfaction with the work environment. Teachers feel respected by one another and by parents, students, and administrators. Teachers perceive the school as having effective administrative leaders.

Recently we interviewed Sarah and Anthony, two teachers we met as undergraduates. Sarah is entering teaching directly after completing her four-year undergraduate teacher education program, and Anthony is a middle-aged career changer entering the teaching ranks and seeking alternative certification. Both are now working as new teachers, and we wanted to learn about the two different school cultures they were working in and how the context was impacting them, their work, and their aspirations to be teacher leaders. The following conversations reflect how they are experiencing these dimensions in two distinctly different school cultures.

*How would you describe the professional development
and learning for new teachers like yourself?
(Developmental Orientation)*

Sarah: I would say we have a pseudo-mentoring program; you know, my mentor is a great person, and she says if you need any help come and see me, but there is no structure, no released time for us to get together, and no specific expectations. So far, I have not participated in any formal professional development activities this first semester except the pre-school day for new teachers.

Anthony: I like that my principal is always sharing articles and books with us; he leads a study group that we can attend on Tuesday mornings if we are interested in discussing the readings with other teachers. I am impressed that the principal frequently stops in and has offered to arrange for me to visit some colleagues' classrooms. My mentor is working with me on the new curriculum we are implementing and has already modeled several lessons with my students while I observed him.

How would you describe the environment in which you work? (Positive Environment)

Sarah: Well, I have decided not to eat lunch in the teachers' lounge any more, as most people are pretty negative. It seems to me that teacher and student input are not valued, and that frustrates teachers very much. I think I can learn some things here, but I probably won't stay forever.

Anthony: We work hard together to meet all of the students' needs. A norm at this school is that we work as a team, so I don't feel alone. I feel that, even as a new teacher, I am in partnership with my colleagues and administrators. My principal makes it clear frequently that our priority is student learning. I think I made a good decision in coming here, and I think transitioning from working in a lab to teaching science has been a good change for me.

How are teachers recognized and rewarded? (Recognition)

Sarah: My assistant principal thanked me for chaperoning the homecoming dance and selling tickets at the football game. Also, my principal gave me positive feedback on a lesson he observed last week, so I felt good about that.

Anthony: What I like is that the administrators value our opinions as teachers, and we are frequently involved in discussions on how to enhance student outcomes. The more experienced teachers also seem to appreciate contributions I make in our team and department meetings, and I enjoy the frequent interactions and even a few pats on the back that are helping me survive in this first year.

How are you encouraged to make improvements or to be innovative? (Autonomy)

Sarah: I am told that resources at my school are pretty limited due to budget cutbacks. I don't have my own classroom yet, so I find it hard to experiment and be creative. Moving all around the school to a different classroom each period makes it difficult to implement the new science curriculum, which requires students to carry out experiments. My department head is happy that my classes are an improvement over the situation last year, when the students had a full time substitute who was not certified in science.

Anthony: I have the support of the literacy coach to help me implement the strategies for reading in the content area, and she is encouraging me to adapt or adjust them for my particular students. She observes my lessons and coaches me on how to improve them as we discuss my own ideas about how the lesson worked. The assistant principal has offered her help if I want to continue to move toward more differentiation in instruction. She says she will help by reviewing my plans ahead of time and coteaching my classes as I learn to manage multiple groups of students working on different levels. We are also using a process called "classroom walkthrough" that involves colleagues walking through our classes and then meeting with us to discuss their observations. I am looking forward to hearing their insights, and I hope to do walkthrough myself next year. It's a lot to learn, but I think all of these initiatives can make a difference with my students.

How would you describe the communication between administration and faculty and among faculty members? (Open Communication)

Sarah: The principal keeps us informed about upcoming events and decisions he has made by issuing a faculty bulletin. I talk often with other science teachers, and my department head has us working together on lesson plans, since many of us are new teachers.

Anthony: Our faculty meetings are for problem solving and discussions among teachers, so I am getting familiar with all of the teachers here. I like working with others outside my team and getting to share our perspectives. I generally feel well informed, as we use e-mail and the school Web site for information sharing. As a school we are open to parents, community members, and business partners who often join us in meetings.

In what ways do you have input or make decisions? (Participation)

Sarah: I can make decisions about my classroom and my students as long as I follow the school and district policy. As I said before, it seems the administration here is not very interested in hearing opinions from teachers and students.

Anthony: We frequently meet when an important decision needs to be made, or sometimes we are requested to give our input or ideas in writing. As a new teacher, I like being involved and look forward to joining the school advisory council perhaps next year. I have heard that experienced teachers are involved in hiring, budgeting, and developing the schedule, so I look forward to that in the future.

How do you collaborate on instructional or student related matters? (Collegiality)

Sarah: I can talk to my mentor and if I need them, I think my administrators would be willing to meet with me. Most of the experienced teachers have been here a long time and seem to keep to themselves pretty much. I feel like a new kid on the block.

Anthony: I have already mentioned the literacy coach, the principal, the assistant principal, and my other department members, with whom I interact frequently. Faculty meetings are structured so we work with other teachers outside our own teams and departments. I recently worked with one of our special education teachers on identifying some strategies to work with a struggling student. I feel like there are many opportunities to discuss, share, and learn with my colleagues in this school.

Our interviews reveal the different school contexts in which Sarah and Anthony find themselves as first-year teachers. It is easy to predict which school culture would be more satisfying to teach in and which might be accomplishing increased student performance. It is also easy to predict which school holds promise for the new teacher in becoming a teacher leader and which would hinder teachers aspiring to leadership.

To assist faculties and administrators in assessing their own school contexts, we developed an instrument, Teacher Leadership School Survey (TLSS; see Resource B), to measure teachers' perceptions of how their own schools reflect these dimensions. We often use this instrument with teachers engaged in our Leadership Development for Teachers course. After teachers respond to the items and graph their scores, we watch as they move around the room. The teachers share their graphs, note the similarities and differences, and discuss the practices in their schools. Teachers from the same school draw to each other like magnets so that they can see if they view their schools in the same way. Discussion of how schools recognize and strengthen teacher leadership can be a springboard for teachers to influence change in the way things are done in their own school settings. Teachers are amazed by the practices that other schools employ, and it is not unusual to hear teachers say, "You mean teachers are involved in making that decision at your school?" or "Your principal encourages teachers to do this at your school?" The TLSS offers an opportunity for teacher leaders to gather teachers' perceptions and to assess how their schools operate with respect to each of the dimensions. Using these data, school administrators and teacher leaders can work together to identify both how they are working effectively and along which dimensions further development is needed to support teacher leadership.

The need for creating truly effective school cultures is more pressing than ever. In order for professional learning communities to thrive in schools, a culture of collaboration must be created; teachers and administrators must work together to achieve their purpose of assuring that all students will learn while focusing on results and making a commitment to student learning (DuFour, 2004). The school context for promoting teacher leadership and thus improving student outcomes is influenced by many factors. We focus in this section on three of the most important factors: (1) the relationships between adults in the school, (2) the actual organizational structure, and (3) the actions of the principal. These three factors are typically under the control of the people within the school and within the school district.

Relationships Among Adults in the School

If the context where teacher leadership takes place is important, then the relationships within that context are pivotal. Gone are the days when a charismatic principal is able to single-handedly provide leadership to a school. Identification of a leadership model to fit the needs in this age of accountability has led to the recognition that leadership must "be relational, not an individual phenomenon" (G. Donaldson, 2006, p. 9). Leadership cannot be successful with a single, heroic leader; rather, the leader must consider how to cultivate relationships so that all teachers, administrators, and parents work together to improve student outcomes. In the schools where there is shared leadership and there is no expectation of heroic leadership from one person, teaching and learning improve (Heller & Firestone, 1994). Fullan (2005) commented that we must "overcome our bias for individualistic solutions" (p. 217) and recognize that no one can do it alone. Of course, principals have the formal power position to lead the school, but they soon recognize that if they are out in front marching ahead without sharing leadership with teachers, or if they are ignoring the collaboration and commitment of teachers, community members, and parents, they will have little success. Principals who hope to accomplish positive outcomes soon recognize that focusing on building relationships both within and outside the school is critical, as is fostering the relationships among the adults within the school.

Given the importance of relationships, Hargreaves and Fullan (1998) suggested that high priority be placed not merely on restructuring the school but rather on "reculturing" it. The goal of reculturing the school is to engage teachers and other stakeholders to work differently together, in more collaborative work cultures. In their guidelines for principals, these authors suggest attention to emotional management, which is ultimately about attending to the relationships within the school (p. 119). Evidence suggests that students learn better when principals, teachers, and others develop collaborative relationships within a professional learning community (Stein, 1998).

Teacher leaders acquire leadership opportunities and the responsibility for building relationships simultaneously. Social interactions influence teacher leadership within a school more than training, experiences, personal characteristics, ability, and the formal structures within the school (A. Hart, 1990). Teachers endeavor to maintain collegial relationships with fellow teachers while assuming leadership roles. These relationships between teacher leaders and other teachers are critical to building a professional community of learners and leaders within the school. Barth (2006) suggested that neither parallel play, nor adversarial relationships, nor congenial relationships will allow professional learning communities to grow in schools. Rather, he suggested that creating a culture of collegiality is needed. A culture of collegiality, he explained, includes talking with one another about practice, sharing craft knowledge, observing one another, and rooting for one another's success.

Principals and teacher leaders must work toward building complementary relationships focused on the mission and goals they mutually strive to accomplish in their schools. Overcoming past stereotypic roles, such as leader as boss, and creatively building new ways of working together will assist both. For teacher leaders, building relationships with colleagues can be even more formidable than working with administrators. The egalitarian norms among teachers do not encourage a teacher to take on leadership roles. These norms respect the privacy of other teachers, and the consequence of violating this expectation may be to suffer rejection from peers. Still, teachers take risks to move beyond their usual roles, because they want to expand their sphere of influence and because they are interested in their own professional growth. An example is a teacher who becomes an advocate for a particular innovation, such as new writing strategies. Once a teacher has a passion for a new idea, the concern about peers' opinions is balanced with the possibilities of connecting with other like-minded colleagues who want to make a difference with students.

The teacher leaders we work with are concerned about their relationships with other teachers. How are they going to influence people who are resistant to change? What happens if they become involved in leadership activities and their friends do not? Why should they take on a task that will alienate them from their colleagues? How do they lead a team of more experienced teachers? Thoughtful conversations need to take place to clarify the roles of teacher leaders in a given school and how the concept fits into the existing culture. Teachers new to their roles as leaders need to have ongoing support and opportunities to problem solve together. Teacher leaders will be aware that their new roles may cause some friction, but they also know that the benefits in improved student performance and increased collegial sharing can outweigh the problems. G. Donaldson (2006) expressed optimism for teacher leaders, because he believes that they possess many assets in building relationships with colleagues, including (a) they are teachers themselves; (b) they still share the work of classroom teaching; (c) teacher leaders often work with small, manageable groups; and (d) they are dependent on their colleagues for their success.

Organizational Structure

The leaders within the school and policymakers outside the school influence the organizational structure. Instead of providing support for collaboration and professional community, schools' structures often wall off teachers and parcel out their time, which contributes to professional distance. Structural changes are needed to promote teacher leadership, according to findings from a study of implementation of change in eight schools (Heller & Firestone, 1994). Schools can be structured in ways that promote autonomous teams of teachers working together. Structural systems may include the way we organize for teaching and learning, the way time and resources are used, the physical structures of the school buildings, the ways we make decisions in schools, the ways information is shared, and the type of incentives offered. Coyle (1997) indicated that the present structure does little to foster the image of teachers as leaders beyond their classrooms and in fact discourages teacher leadership; not much has changed significantly in many schools in terms of structure since Coyle's comment over a decade ago.

It is amazing that teacher leadership is possible in schools as they are currently structured. Fortunately, promising alternatives to current structures are emerging. Schools are utilizing approaches such as "houses" within larger schools, where groups of students and a cohort of teachers work together. Also, a continuous-progress arrangement, in which a team of teachers stays with a multiage group of children for more than one year, is another structure that allows for flexibility. Schools have also restructured their staffing patterns. For example, some schools have implemented the practice of "pushing in" special assistance to students within their classrooms or teams rather than pulling out students for services (Darling-Hammond, 1997). These structures can support teacher leadership by giving teachers options for how they plan and go about their work.

Other structural changes can easily be made within a school. Many schools plan faculty meetings that engage teachers in collaboratively discussing teaching and learning rather than the typical principal-dominated meeting with a long list of announcements. Arranging common planning time for teachers encourages collaboration on curriculum and instructional matters. Rearranging the school schedule to free a team of teachers to review test data, to discuss student work, to find resources for an upcoming thematic unit, or for observing a demonstration lesson in another team teacher's classroom are all examples of promising structural modifications. Often, with a little creative thought and openness to doing things differently, structures can be modified to enhance the chances that teachers can learn and lead together. These minor changes are helpful, but substantive changes in school structures are needed to relieve the stress teacher leaders feel when they try to balance their commitment to their students in their classrooms with their work leading others.

Structures within and outside the schools cannot be overlooked. Systems for recognition, communication, and participation must be explicit in their design. For example, teacher leaders need to know how decisions are really made in a school. As more teachers become familiar with the way to get things done, more leadership will emerge. To build a positive environment for teacher leadership to function within these systems demands resourceful ways of building structures for teachers to learn, lead, and collaborate. Teachers will be motivated to remain in leadership roles if they experience greater control over their work and if the organizational structures support their efforts to make change. A recent study of five schools (Beachum & Dentith, 2004) found that a central theme explaining the presence of teacher leadership across the schools was that there were specific school structures and organizational patterns that were put into place to support teacher leaders. These schools were structured so that teachers worked in strong and functioning teams, and teachers were given time to plan, talk about their teaching, and work on problems and new initiatives. Practices in these five schools included supporting many teacher-initiated changes; likewise, administrators embraced innovation and were perceived as open to change. Teachers felt they had autonomy and that their ideas were heard and respected.

The constant pressures of national and state mandates and the demand of accountability for outcomes tempt principals to keep busy attending to the daily tasks of attending district meetings, handling complaints from parents and students, and assuring student disruptions do not take away valuable instructional time. All of these tasks are important, yet the time spent working with teachers to establish viable communication networks, effective decision making groups, and celebrations of success give the school more valuable returns.

One of the most frequently mentioned problems with organizational structures is that teachers don't have time in the school day for collaboration and leadership activities. For example, in a 2006 survey in North Carolina schools, over 29% of respondents indicated that time was the working condition most important to improving student learning (Hirsch, Emerick, Church, & Fuller, 2006b). This was true also in survey results for 2002 and 2004; time continued to be the most problematic working condition for teachers across the state. Similarly, the National Staff Development Council (von Frank, 2008) advocates that 25% of a teacher's contract time in every work week should be spent on professional development. Teachers must be provided with adequate time if they are to meet the challenges of acquiring best practices, teaching an ever more diverse population, and changing curriculum to meet 21st-century standards. In Resource C, we offer a further discussion of time and provide strategies for providing time for teacher leadership work.

Actions of the Principal

Looking historically at the evolution of the principal's role helps in understanding how the actions of the principal have had to change over time to provide a culture supportive of teacher leadership. In the late 1980s, we believed that if schools were to be effective, principals must be instructional leaders (Lezotte & Jacoby, 1990). Meanwhile, they also had to respond to the multiple demands of their school district and the state. They were expected to be good *managers* by attending to all the details and completing paperwork on time, good *supervisors* of teachers and noninstructional staff, and good *bosses* who kept the school faculty motivated, compliant, and cooperative. When we worked in the mid-1980s with a principal development program in a large urban district, much of the focus was on principals' responsibilities, such as budgeting, teacher evaluation, scheduling the students, and managing the school facility.

In the 1990s, shared decision making became the prevalent movement. The shared leadership initiatives held promise for principals willing to involve teachers and other stakeholders as active members in the decision making process. Data from a study of exemplary leaders in Georgia suggest that principals as facilitative leaders contribute significantly to teachers' overall sense of empowerment (Blasé & Blasé, 1997). Similarly, results from the School Restructuring Study (King, Louis, Marks, & Peterson, 1996) showed that actions of principals have shifted from more directive to more shared approaches. Principals in schools that shared decision making took action that encouraged teacher leadership and contributed to a focus on the intellectual quality of student work. This study suggested that principals in successful schools nurtured decision making by teachers, encouraged experimentation, took entrepreneurial initiative, and buffered the school from external demands. The vision of shared leadership reflects principals' taking action to engage teachers in leadership; however, the reality was that many teachers still remained out of the decision making loop. A decade ago, only about a third of teachers perceived that they influenced major decisions, such as those made about curriculum and discipline (Shen, 1998). Today, teachers who make hundreds of classroom decisions on a daily basis still find themselves not being involved in making schoolwide decisions to the extent they would like to be involved.

More recently, ideas related to the work of the effective principal have become even more aligned with our concept of teacher leadership. When studying the principalship, many educators are now advocates of leadership based on thinking of schools as professional learning communities, and these communities are being defined in terms of agreement among faculty members on shared values, beliefs, and commitments. Sergiovanni (2000) recommended that principals direct their efforts toward making shared values explicit, and these shared values become sources for informal norms that govern behavior. As community members, teachers respond to their duties and obligations in keeping with the school community's informal norm system. These connections allow principals to rely less on external control. The result is that teachers become increasingly self-managed. Harris and Spillane (2008) described distributed leadership as an alternative way to think about leadership in schools; they suggested that leadership practice is constructed in the interactions between leaders, followers, and their situations. Their view is that leadership incorporates the work of many individuals who have a hand in leading the school. Because of the complexity of change and the great need to improve instructional practice, principals today soon find they must rely on a variety of teachers who bring expertise in the their subject areas and recent classroom experience to model the way for others. In these situations, teacher leaders emerge and assume responsibilities depending on their knowledge and competence.

Today, we recognize that a main way to differentiate effective from less effective principals is that effective principals spend time actively involved in curricular and instructional issues, while the less effective spend most of their time on organizational maintenance and student discipline (Cotton, 2003). The principals who are engaged in real school change recognize that every teacher can be a leader in partnership with the principal and that roles of teaching, learning, and leading can be played by everyone in organizations that are, in the words of Lieberman and Miller (1999), "leadership dense" (p. 46).

As we work with principals today, the leadership conversations have changed, but potential principals still expect the graduate school or professional development providers to prepare them in the technical responsibilities. Often, these future leaders at first believe their success rests only on managing the facility, building the budget, or creating the master schedule. Our approach to their development, however, is focused on a more complex form of leadership that emphasizes values and beliefs, shared vision, school culture, teacher leadership, professional learning communities, and transforming schools to focus on teaching and learning so that all students can learn. As important as mastery of the technical and managerial skills may be, today's principals must reconsider how to use the technical tasks of the work of schooling to their advantage in partnering with the school's teacher leaders in transforming the teaching and learning that occurs.

Another contemporary role for the principal is to serve as a buffer for obstacles from outside the school. These obstacles may come from district staff, parents, community members, or other external forces, such as special interest groups. The principals of successful schools negotiate with the larger system (Goldring & Rallis, 1993) and develop liaisons with powerful individuals to diminish these barriers for the school. Teachers may not even be aware of the efforts principals make to shield them from unpleasant information that could lessen the teachers' enthusiasm to lead. One teacher leader we spoke with recently told of being given the leadership task of raising math scores in her high school. She was quite surprised that she needed to spend a lot of her time defending the plans that she and the teachers agreed upon to the district math supervisory staff. She reported that her principal backed her and her colleagues; the results were positive, and the students made large gains in math in just one year.

As teacher leaders move beyond their classrooms and schools, they are often surprised by the political nature of a school district or a community. That is, teachers say that the professional climate in their schools can make or break their leadership efforts, and most of them see the principal as a primary factor in creating a good professional climate. If the principal openly embraces shared leadership and encourages their participation in decision making, then teachers are more comfortable advocating for important issues. In addition, schools are relatively unstable environments. New programs are phased in, old programs are phased out, and teachers find themselves in different buildings, new school communities, and, of course, working with a fresh group of students who have different needs than the previous group of students had. This change factor appears to be a significant force in teachers' abilities to serve as effective teacher leaders in their schools. A teacher leader we know developed a plan to address her concerns about a program, only to learn shortly thereafter that the program would be phased out. Another teacher leader, who expected to take her turn as interdisciplinary team leader for her grade, spent the summer planning ways to improve the team's effectiveness, but at the beginning of the school year, she was instead switched to a new team that did not have the need to meet regularly and was chaired by someone else.

As previously mentioned, time to implement the plans is a challenge for teacher leaders, particularly when the success of an innovation requires time for conversations, collaborative planning and problem solving, professional development, evaluation, and more. The issue of time is frequently not addressed by administrators with teachers; it is simply understood that teachers must put in the additional time and energy required to do something innovative. One teacher leader shared comments that reflect the concerns of many: "It's a lot of work for me. It's a lot more work than it would have been if I had just sat back and taught the same thing I've been teaching for seven years." She concluded that she would not have gone forward in implementing her plan if she had not been totally committed to the idea.

Finally, Moller and Pankake (2006) suggested that the actions of principals to provide supportive conditions is a key factor in encouraging shared leadership and nurturing teacher leadership roles within professional learning communities. The principal supports teacher leadership by actively listening to teachers, by assuming responsibility for knowing about teaching and learning in the school, and by being consistent in the follow-through on shared decisions made in the school. Many sources point to the importance of the actions of the principal, which are critical to creating a school context that is supportive of the work of teacher leaders.

Conclusion

The success of teacher leadership depends on the context in which it takes place. School leaders with exemplary schools make teacher leadership a priority and take risks to provide teacher leaders what they need to succeed. This does not happen by chance; it is a conscious effort by these leaders to design an environment that is supportive of all learning, including teacher leadership development.

Schools that are providing a context that supports teacher leadership pay attention to measurable dimensions that are important to building a context for teacher leadership. Explicit efforts must be made to develop the relationships between adults in the school, the actual organizational structures must be created, and the principal's actions must be aligned. Each of these affects the success of teacher leadership and ultimately affects student outcomes.

School principals who devote energy to teacher leadership make capital gains in their own power. More is accomplished, students do better, the community is less critical of the school, and the teachers are more satisfied. The result is better use of people, and this in turn influences student outcomes. Teacher leadership benefits the principals and the teachers, but most important, it benefits the students in the building. Given the appropriate context in the school, teacher leaders can and do influence teaching and learning.

APPLICATION CHALLENGES

For Teachers

1. If money and resources were unlimited, how would you structure and organize to assure teachers could lead and all students could

learn? Talk with interested colleagues about the organizational structures that are needed to make teacher leadership a priority.

2. List the kinds of decisions teachers make within your school, and then list the kinds of decisions you would like to see teachers make within your school. Examine each item on the lists and ask two questions: Is this decision relevant to teachers? Do teachers have or can they gain expertise to make this decision? If the answer is yes to both, continue to exert influence to get teachers involved in those decisions.

For Principals

1. Collaboration among teachers is key to improving teaching and learning in schools. Analyze where and how collaboration occurs in your building. Seek insights from teachers about what you can do to step up the collaboration among teachers. Ask also if you are in any way hindering collaboration.

2. Teachers taking on leadership roles may be suspect, and relations with peers may be negatively impacted. Consider how you can introduce the teacher leadership roles effectively, and provide ongoing encouragement, support, and problem solving help to assist teacher leaders to be accepted in positive ways within the school's current culture.

For Superintendents and District-Level Administrators

1. Systems thinking can help leaders recognize that people (especially teachers) are usually not the problem—systems are the problem. Instead of blaming, think about how you can examine your processes, procedures, and policies to detect how the way you are doing things evolved. Then decide upon necessary changes to the system and the organizational practices to support teacher leadership in improving student outcomes.

2. When teachers' abilities are acknowledged and they are treated in democratic ways, they probably find it easier to do the same for their students. What are you doing to help make the shift from a bureaucratic view of the teacher as executor of district decisions to the teacher as decision maker with expertise and potential to make choices at the school and classroom level? Be honest with yourselves as a group of supervisory personnel in discussing your beliefs and assessing your actions.

For College and University Professors

1. Consider using the Teacher Leader School Survey (TLSS) (See Resource B) to gather data on how teacher leadership is being supported in the schools in which you place interns. Engage your students in looking for positive examples of each of the dimensions on the TLSS as they observe and work in schools. Then discuss these best practices in your university classes.

2. Assign an Internet search to your undergraduate students to find and learn about models of schools of the future. Direct their attention in particular to the relationships and organizational structures that might exist in high-performing schools of the future.

6

Influencing
Others Through
Teacher Leadership

*I believe we'd be best served to think of [school reform] more as a
giant science experiment where we formulate strategies for figuring
out what we think and believe is best for kids, learn how to best
explain that, figure out who the target audience of influence should
be and then try to impact that audience.*

Marsha Ratzel, Middle School Teacher Leader

We have all observed young children who are beginning to
learn they have influence over significant adults in their lives.
At this stage, they begin to experiment with their voices: gurgling,
shrieking, and beginning to form their first words. There is a look of
surprise and satisfaction on their faces when they recognize that
through using their voices they can influence people and circumstances around them. Similarly, when teachers' awareness of their
roles as leaders is raised, and they find their leadership voices for the
first time, they begin to see that their voices are heard by their colleagues, by the parents, and by people in the community. Teacher leaders

with influencing skills impact their own practice, their colleagues' professional learning, and broader instructional programs, priorities, and policies. Teachers' voices are often silent, yet their perspectives need to be heard by all stakeholders attempting to improve schools. Ultimately this work has the potential to make a difference in the bottom line—student learning.

Teacher leaders can make a difference in schools through the actions they take. In our work, we hear hundreds of stories of teacher leaders who have influenced positive changes in their schools. What do all the stories we have heard have in common? Teacher leaders are able to influence situations in their schools through their modeling of their own effective practice, their collaboration with others, and their involvement in decision making and problem solving. Their work as leaders involves them with opportunities for interaction, observation, and reflection, which provide them with learning opportunities to improve their own practice. York-Barr and Duke (2004), examining two decades of research on teacher leadership, asserted that one of the clearest effects of teacher leadership is, in fact, growth and learning among the teachers themselves. Teachers who are leaders influence their colleagues and often assist in making changes in practices at the classroom and school levels. As they gain a broader perspective, beyond just their individual classrooms, these teachers have firsthand knowledge of improvements that are needed and how to address them. Teacher leaders experiment and learn to collaboratively solve the problems in the context of the school with which they are thoroughly familiar.

Influence With Instructional Competence

Barth (2001) pointed out that teacher expertise about teaching and learning is needed to lead instructional improvement. Snell and Swanson (2000) in their study of ten teacher leaders found that "expertise [was] the foundational dimension of teacher leadership, for it served to establish the credibility of these teachers as exemplars, which, thereby opened the door for them to function as instructional leaders" (p. 19). Through their expertise, teacher leaders model effective practice, mentor colleagues, and, through collaboration with others, break down the isolation that keeps many teachers stuck behind their classroom doors repeating the same instructional strategies regardless of the outcomes. The first component in our definition of teacher leadership is that the teacher leads *within* the classroom through excellence in teaching.

With this competence, teachers can learn how to influence others in order to take advantage of this resource. An example of the importance of engaging outstanding teachers is reflected in Proposition 5 developed by the National Board for Professional Teaching Standards. This proposition states

---

Proposition 5: Teachers Are Members of Learning Communities.

NBCTs [National Board certified teachers] collaborate with others to improve student learning.

They are leaders and actively know how to seek and build partnerships with community groups and businesses.

They work with other professionals on instructional policy, curriculum development and staff development.

They can evaluate school progress and the allocation of resources in order to meet state and local education objectives.

They know how to work collaboratively with parents to engage them productively in the work of the school. (National Board for Professional Teaching Standards, 2008b)

With this instructional expertise, teachers are usually perceived by their colleagues as credible. Because teacher leaders may not find themselves in situations that give them position power, they usually do not operate from a position of authority. The teacher leaders' personal power comes from the perception of their competence by other teachers. A principal spoke of a teacher leader, saying, "She is still a peer to many, but an expert on our campus."

How Teachers Influence

Teachers influence others through a variety of routes. After successfully using a teaching strategy, a teacher may become an advocate who shares the approach with other teachers. Lieberman and Miller (2004) suggested that teachers must try things out themselves in their classrooms before they are willing to share with others. When they talk with colleagues, they influence them, and this outcome is powerful, because teachers are working from personal experience and are advocating new methods based on what appears to work with their students.

A principal told us of how a special education teacher influenced colleagues: "Our special education program will be in the classroom next year, not a pull-out program. She is a believer in it." This teacher had a passion for her idea, and she influenced other teachers, who may have been reluctant to make a change or modify practice.

Much of the support in the literature for the impact of teacher leadership is descriptive rather than offering evidence of measurable results, yet there are efforts to gain this evidence of the impact resulting from teacher leadership (Mangin & Stoelinga, 2008). Meanwhile, here are descriptions of the power of influence gathered through our work with teacher leaders.

- A teacher leader serving as a full time mentor to new teachers in disadvantaged schools recognized the importance of his relationship with his principals. He influenced the staff development director in the district to plan a yearly session for principals and mentors to initiate their working relationships and to plan for how they would interact and work together to help teachers.
- Several teacher leaders studied effective professional development and then systematically redesigned a yearlong schoolwide professional development approach designed to increase the use of technology in classrooms. Designing the sessions, facilitating the grade-level groups, and strategizing about the follow-up were all actions that the teacher leaders engaged in to implement a long-term, results-oriented approach to professional development.
- In another school, teacher leaders recognized the need to offer help and assistance to the large number of new noncertified teachers who joined their faculty each year. The action they decided upon was to arouse the interest of their peers in learning about effective mentoring and to seek volunteers from among the experienced faculty to mentor each new teacher. Afterschool support meetings were held for problem solving with the new teachers as a group. The mentors periodically invited the new teachers to observe in their classes.
- A teacher leader who served as a grade-level team leader took action to influence the principal on behalf of all the team leaders in the school. Fortunately, the principal welcomed the conversation about how he could improve communication with team leaders and teachers by asking for input and providing adequate time for their work to take place. The teacher leader also helped the principal to see that the role of team leader was not clear in this particular school. What were the expectations? What was reasonable, given the time teachers had outside of their classrooms to

devote to the role? These and other questions were resolved through dialogue with the principal in the next team leaders' meeting.

- Another teacher leader was given the responsibility to improve reading instruction in the primary grades. Through a study group, she and other members built their knowledge of how to teach reading. She built trust with her peers and offered her help; then she was invited to come into teachers' classes to teach demonstration lessons in reading. Some teachers in her building developed confidence from watching her model instructional strategies, and eventually they tried out the new reading strategies themselves. She was available to plan with them and to coach them upon request.

It is predictable that teacher leaders would influence teaching and learning, but they can also contribute to other aspects of schooling. Teacher leaders can affect policy decisions, secure community resources, and work with parents. The range of possibilities is endless. Successful school leaders help teachers to find their passion or a niche of influence. Teachers then become advocates and attract other teachers to the change effort.

To take advantage of this potential, we must prepare teachers to be effective in influencing others. Teacher leaders who use their skills to influence their colleagues may gain the confidence to apply their skills with parents, with the principal, with the district staff, and with members of the larger educational community. With an awareness of their personal strengths and developmental needs and an appreciation for the context in which they are working, the third component in leadership development for teachers is learning influencing strategies and considering the question, "How do I lead?" (Figure 6.1).

Influencing Strategies

Developmental opportunities for teacher leaders should build teacher leaders' skills to influence other individuals. The skill sets that support teacher leaders are listening, facilitating groups, and learning techniques to negotiate with administrators, other teachers, parents, or other key stakeholders in order to influence positive action.

Teachers need new skills if they are to be successful in taking on the roles and responsibilities of leading their peers. Moving into these roles without skills can be treacherous for teachers who are anxious about influencing their peers. Almost 20 years ago, Goodlad (1990) pointed out that "there is irresponsibility in significantly expanding

Figure 6.1   Influencing Others

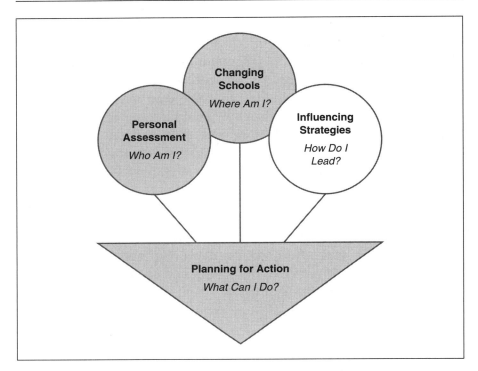

teachers' authority without educating them to use it well" (p. 27). Potential teacher leaders can begin to develop the knowledge and skills for having influence during their undergraduate and graduate programs. Also, districts and schools can continue this developmental process throughout the teachers' careers. Weiss, Cambone, and Wyeth (1992) suggested that teachers' new roles and relations will present challenges; teacher leaders will have to be prepared to negotiate, manage conflicts, and come to decisions with others—all the more reason that developing the influencing capabilities of all teacher leaders is essential.

Listening Skills

Some people believe they need to be able to provide answers if they are in leadership roles. We counsel teacher leaders to think about listening rather than telling if they want to be successful in their leadership. Teacher leaders who develop these skills report they become more influential by using good listening techniques with peers and others. We often ask how many participants in the teacher leadership development sessions have had any preparation in undergraduate or graduate programs in listening. Fewer than 10% in most groups report skill development opportunities in listening. Yet, teacher leaders tell us that developing these skills is one of the most valuable parts of their leadership learning. They describe using their skills diagnostically as well as citing changes in their behavior in problem solving situations and in relating to their colleagues. Listening with empathy is reported as critical to their newly acquired leadership roles. A teacher leader stated, "By actually hearing and being certain I heard what I thought I heard, I can better serve the teachers."

We introduce teacher leaders to a model we call FLEX (Figure 6.2), an acronym for remembering their newly honed listening skills. As we review the listening skills, the teachers realize that they know these skills but rarely use them effectively. This is especially true with the first skill, *focus on the speaker without judging or formulating your response.* The next skill is *listen using open body language,* which is violated by actions such as crossed arms or sitting behind a desk. Then we encourage teachers to *empathize by trying to see through the other person's eyes.* This is a crucial skill for influencing others and reflects the teacher's ability to work with diverse perspectives. Finally, we suggest that the teacher *examine nonverbal cues, and explore words for meaning and feeling.* So often we are anxious about getting our viewpoints expressed, and in these situations we may overlook these clues to the other person's perspective. Teacher leaders practice these skills through discussions of educational issues that are crucial for them. Then they give and receive feedback to one another as they practice the skills.

Teacher leaders interact with colleagues within and outside their buildings, with parents and community leaders, with college and

Figure 6.2   Listening Skills

F ocus on the speaker without judging or formulating your response.

L isten using open body language.

E mpathize by trying to see through the other person's eyes.

E **X** amine nonverbal cues and explore words for meaning and feeling.

university faculty members, and with legislators and other policy makers. All of these interactions require excellent listening skills as part of the process of being able to influence others. Our follow-up studies reveal that teacher leaders used the skills beyond their professional roles: 44% reported the skills were used in civic and church work, and 41% reported using the skills with spouses, family members, and children (Hewitt-Gervais, 1996).

Group Skills

Teachers' experience in their work on committees and teams reveals that learning to work in groups requires new skills. Teachers who were prepared for their roles in classrooms decades ago traditionally did not develop skills in facilitating groups of adults. Using these skills empowers teacher leaders to behave in new ways to influence actions toward issues of concern. Skillful teacher leaders can help the group solve problems, make decisions, and manage the inevitable conflicts. Opportunities to develop the expertise to fill the roles of a facilitator, a recorder, and a reporter in small groups can improve a teacher's capacity to lead.

Hearing All Voices

A teacher acting as a *facilitator* can make sure everyone in a group has an opportunity to speak, can make suggestions to keep a group on time and on task, and can focus on the process, not the content, of the discussion.

A teacher acting as a *recorder* for a group can listen to all ideas presented and accurately capture the key ideas being offered; doing so includes and values everyone's ideas.

A teacher acting as a *reporter* can share the group's ideas by summarizing the main ideas from the discussion while using gestures and body language effectively.

We find behavior-modeling approaches (Taylor, Russ-Eft, & Chan, 2005) to be useful strategies in developing these group skills. In this method, participants see a new skill modeled in person or by video, learn a series of steps or behaviors that make up the skill, and then prepare for and practice the skill. After performing the skills, the teachers gain feedback from the others about their performance. We find that behavior-modeling strategies are an excellent methodology for aiding educators in developing new skills. As with all professional development, teachers must have follow-up and support as they attempt to use them in their school settings.

Many teachers have reported on the use of the group skills in their classrooms with students and in their leadership roles with colleagues (Hart & Segesta, 1994). Here are a few examples:

- One teacher shared how she used her new skills while serving as chairperson of the school curriculum revision team.
- Another teacher shared how he was facilitating his team's meetings and said that the group skills worked much more efficiently than traditional parliamentary procedures previously used.
- A technology resource teacher described how she used her skills to facilitate a recent planning session for the implementation of Smart Boards in classrooms in her school.
- A literacy coach who meets frequently with new teachers explained that she is now able to keep the whole group involved in sharing ideas in a shorter of time.
- A special education coordinator described her success with facilitating conferences that involved administrators, school psychologists, teachers, and parents.

Many teacher leaders describe how meetings in their schools rarely result in positive outcomes. After learning these facilitative skills, they recognize how they can take action to improve the meetings for everyone involved.

Negotiating Skills

This skill set helps teacher leaders develop strategies in order to collaborate with people who may have different perspectives. Since professional development schools, site-based management, shared decision making, and involvement in collaborative relationships have become more common, teacher leaders are being called upon to influence peer teachers, principals, district staff, and parents and sometimes even university professors. Teacher leaders can learn to formulate and present their viewpoints on current issues or situations related to school change in order to influence other stakeholders. Many teacher leaders understand the use of these skills to be not manipulative but rather positive strategies to encourage collaboration and involvement.

Preparing to Influence

Taking the time to thoroughly prepare for a meeting saves time in the long term and honors the other person in the conversation.

Often, teacher leaders wonder why they are unsuccessful in influencing others, and, in many cases, the reason is that they are not prepared to talk about their ideas and did not predict what the other person's perspective might be. We use the following guidelines in our leadership development initiatives to help teachers prepare to influence others in more positive ways.

Guideline #1: Identify own position. Preparation includes thinking through the teacher's own position on the issue or situation. Teachers are encouraged to write out their positions to help them clarify their beliefs. When teachers write out their positions, they may find they do not have enough information to present their case.

Guideline #2: Gather data. Then we suggest the teachers use data from personal experience and research findings to enhance and support their positions. Using data from research requires that teachers inform themselves about what educational research has to offer them. It may also encourage them to take on action research projects or to use other data-gathering processes to find support for their positions.

Guideline #3: Identify the needs of self and others. Next, the teachers think about their own needs and interests in the situation and try to predict the needs and interests of the people they intend to influence. To achieve common goals, the wants of all those involved must be satisfied. Teacher leaders spend time thinking about how their personal needs and the needs of the people they are trying to influence may be the same or different.

Many teachers report that they find the preparation to be an essential tool in their work with school improvement teams, curriculum committees, and other school-site work groups. A teacher leader from Georgia shared with us how she used her preparation planning steps when she met with the superintendent to discuss her ideas on teacher retention and how district policy might be changed. Another teacher leader described how she now approaches her principal by first developing a plan of how to influence him.

Steps to Influencing Others

Teacher leaders can become skilled in influencing others with professional learning, practice, and feedback. These skills help to influence students, other teachers, parents, or administrators; they are applicable in many settings. The six steps we suggest to teacher leaders when using these skills include:

Step 1: Clearly and confidently state your own position. Teachers need to see themselves as leaders who can make a difference and whose opinions are important. Practicing being confident and clear in the presentation of a position is essential to success.

Step 2: Use data to support the position taken. Data collected during the preparation stage are useful in building the confidence of the teacher leader to influence others. Although most data simply support the teacher leaders' intuitive beliefs about their practice, it is comforting when one's position can be validated through research or the experiences of others.

Step 3: Seek out and understand the perspective of others. While preparing, teacher leaders predicted what would be the needs of those they were seeking to influence. Now they probe to find out if their assumptions were correct.

Step 4: Identify what is at stake for both parties. To move toward agreement, teacher leaders need to elicit what the perspectives of others are. Examining what would make all parties feel satisfied is essential if there is to be sincere support of the final decision.

Step 5: Generate options for a specific situation or problem resolution. The ability to get all the options into the open helps move toward a decision. An option offered may differ from the teacher leader's original proposal yet may become the best solution for everyone involved.

Step 6: Reach agreement. Reaching agreement with a variety of stakeholders strengthens the influence teacher leaders can have on school change efforts. The feeling of success comes when the teacher leader successfully works with others to meet everyone's needs and promote change in schools to improve student learning.

Two communication models shared previously in this book help teacher leaders their conversations with others. First, we shared the ADS model (see Chapter 4), in which teachers learn to *acknowledge their differences, disclose their values and views,* and *seek to understand and include others.* Successful influencing involves collaboration with people who may have different perspectives, and the ADS model reminds teacher leaders that openness can lead to a more productive outcome. In addition, the FLEX model for listening is a powerful tool for engaging others in meaningful discussions about the issue the teacher leader hopes to influence. In our work with teacher leaders who are practicing these skills, we encourage them to introduce their issue briefly and then to listen to the other person's perspective on the same issue. Spending time using effective listening skills with other people may reveal that the person is already supportive of the ideas, or it may lead to a new perspective for the teacher leader. This gives the teacher leader an advantage in understanding the possible solutions to a pressing problem.

Teacher leaders use influencing strategies for specific purposes, and these are usually linked to their concern about a problem or issue in the school. Skills are helpful, but unless the teacher leader has an action plan, the outcomes may be haphazard.

Teacher Leader Action in Schools

The final component of the model we propose for developing teacher leaders helps them answer the question, "What can I do?" (see Figure 6.3). The development of teacher leaders through the first three components of the model—*Personal Assessment, Changing Schools,* and *Influencing Strategies*—prepares them to take action. Building on personal and school visions teachers have for the future, as well as data they have gathered based on needs they recognize for improvement, helps teacher leaders to focus on specific actions in a leadership role.

Figure 6.3   Taking Action

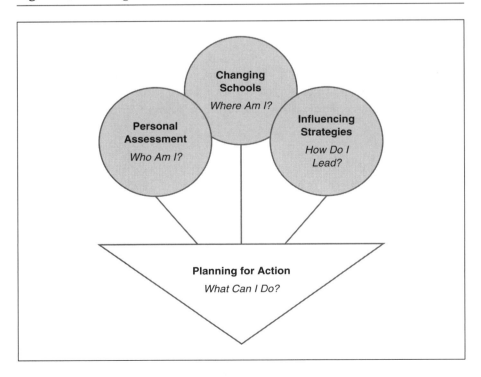

Increasingly there is pressure for teacher leadership to be focused on student learning with measurable outcomes. Teacher leaders cannot simply be involved and influence others without accountability for school outcomes. In fact, we added being *responsible for achieving outcomes* to our definition of teacher leadership. One way to take on this responsibility is to learn how to develop an effective action plan. Although these plans are often called *action research* or *teacher research*, this is not the academic research feared or dismissed by too many practitioners. These are practical ways to make a difference regarding an issue of major concern to the teacher leader.

Teacher leaders benefit from a job-embedded learning experience of developing an Influencing Action Plan. Based on our belief that teacher leaders need structures to be successful in influencing practice in their schools and districts, we provide these teachers with an opportunity to learn new influencing skills by carrying out a real-life project in their schools or school districts. Teacher leaders engage in drafting a proposal for their Influencing Action Plan that builds the teacher leader's skills and confidence. Figure 6.4 describes the steps.

The first step in creating the Influencing Action Plan involves teacher leaders determining the issues for which they are willing to take action by contributing their energy and time. Teacher leaders think about evidence they have to prove their concern is a problem and then proceed to collect formal and informal data about the issue. In the next step, teacher leaders look outside their schools to find examples of solutions to the problem used in other schools or by other teachers. This verifies that the problem can be solved and allows the teacher leader to determine the feasibility of investing in a realistic issue that has the potential to be resolved. The third step involves the teacher leader in setting goals for improvement to clarify the results that are anticipated. At this stage, the teacher leader seeks feedback from colleagues and communicates about the issue with a formal leader in the school, usually the principal. With these sources of feedback considered, the teacher leader refines the focus and goals of the plan before proceeding.

The final three steps of the Influencing Action Plan help the teacher examine outside resources and practices inside the school in order to develop a tentative plan of action. In the fourth step, the teacher leader investigates what strategies have been used to try to solve the problem and the success of these existing or past strategies. Next, the teacher leader reaches outside to identify research and best practices used in other schools and school districts that can contribute to an understanding of how to proceed. Finally, the teacher leader selects strategies and develops action steps. The teacher leader

Figure 6.4   Influencing Action Plan (IAP) Steps

STEP 1: Current Information About the Issue: How do you know this is a problem?

- Explanation of issue
- Rationale for selecting the issue
- Narrative description of context, including a summary of student and faculty demographics as well as a description of the school culture and leadership information
- Data to support your concerns: student performance, attendance, disciplinary concerns, teacher concerns, and other information (can be either qualitative or quantitative)
- Your position (and general information about you) and your role in advocating an approach to this issue

STEP 2: Likelihood of Addressing the Issue: How do you know that this issue can be effectively addressed?

- Comparative data (e.g., data from similar schools, county/state/national data) and characteristics/needs of the learner in relation to this issue (e.g., research on how learners like those in your school best learn math)

STEP 3: Ideal Situation: What would be the ideal situation?

- Ideal behaviors or levels of performance; benchmarks for the learner

STEP 4: Existing Strategies: What is known about strategies that are being used to address this issue now?

- Existing strategies and programs in place to address the issue, whether they are or are not effective

STEP 5: Research and Best Practices: What is known about other strategies that could address this issue?

- Research and best practices related to the issue (may include interviews and information gained from other schools with programs that address your issue)
- Based on the research, the ideal teaching and learning environment: How will you adapt curriculum, schedule, and other relevant concerns to address the issue?

STEP 6: Selected Strategies and Action Steps: What strategies will be used to reach the ideal situation?

- Process to promote IAP in your school/district and your role in this process
- Key stakeholders and strategies you will use to influence them in advocating for your issue
- Professional learning needs of those who will implement the plan

---

Source: Adapted from Calhoun, 2002.

engages in action planning by considering the role he or she will play, the resources needed, what the timeline will be, and who key stakeholders are and how they might be influenced as well as how success will be measured.

Action research is a growing phenomenon, as teacher leaders realize that they can use their learning not only to impact their own situation but also to influence others toward improved practice. Here are a few examples of outcomes from Influencing Action Plans developed by teacher leaders:

- Collaborated with fifth grade teachers to integrate social studies topics into art lessons
- Established first multiage classroom in an elementary school
- Moved high school–age, trainable mentally disabled students from middle school classroom to the high school
- Formed consistent discipline procedures for students when they are in special classes (e.g., art, music)
- Promoted team building for staff in newly consolidated school

Seeking assistance from colleagues and others in formulating plans as they venture into formerly uncharted territories is reassuring for many teacher leaders. Once the plans are complete, teacher leaders are motivated to make a difference by taking action in their school settings; then they take responsible steps to carry out the actions, knowing they and others are accountable for the results.

Conclusion

Teachers, if afforded opportunities, can increase effectiveness in the public schools. Influencing by teacher leaders is not without its difficulties, but it is certainly worth the efforts. Dilemmas teacher leaders face as they influence others may include (a) inflexible team members; (b) unwillingness of other teachers to tackle tough decisions, such as school budgets and allocation of scarce resources; and (c) lack of follow-through by principals on teacher leaders' decisions. Still, progress is being made in providing teachers more opportunities to influence, but there is much work to be done before teachers are legitimate contributors to meaningful decision making. School leaders are moving toward restructuring the work within the schools to involve those closest to the actual work—the teachers—in making decisions.

This approach places teacher leaders in more relevant roles and puts the decision making closer to the students. We believe it will improve student outcomes in the long run.

Evidence of growth in the acknowledgment of teacher leadership as a valuable asset is the growth of formal roles that primarily focus on instructional leadership. Although we applaud the recognition of teacher leadership potential, we are concerned that these teachers are asked to take on roles without preparation and support in school cultures that are often hostile to their work. There are specific strategies that school leaders, district administrators, and others can implement to provide a safer entry into the dilemmas of teacher leadership.

APPLICATION CHALLENGES

For Teachers

1. Reflect on the many ways in which teachers have influence at your school site. Consider how their work has impact at the *whole school level,* such as serving on a school improvement team; the *professional development level,* such as performing demonstration lessons in other teachers' classrooms; or the *instructional level,* such as sharing with a new teacher how to use the technology for classroom activities. Share your findings with others in advocating for teacher leaders and the potential impact on student outcomes.

2. Think about the burning issues for you related to your students. What concerns you the most and inhibits their learning? Examples might be nutrition and childhood obesity, homeless children, secondary students who must work to help support their siblings, or drug and alcohol use. Consider how you might influence one of these issues by working together with teacher leaders in your school and using your influencing skills.

For Principals and Assistant Principals

1. Observe team, department, or faculty meetings with an eye to how effectively teachers' voices are heard in your school. Examine ways in which teachers' influence can be increased within your school and how you can encourage teachers to effectively contribute to problem solving and decision making.

2. Using teacher expertise is at the heart of assuring quality teachers in every classroom and making improvements in teaching

and learning. Survey teachers to ascertain the specific areas of expertise they recognize in themselves as well as among their colleagues. Use these findings to plan ways to engage teachers in modeling instructional practices for others, in sharing best practices, or in identifying mentors for new teachers.

For Superintendents and District Staff

1. Given that it is commonly understood that greater employee participation leads to greater commitment and more effective decisions in an organization, how might you more fully engage teacher leaders in influencing policy and practice related to teaching and learning? Find additional ways to enhance the use of teacher leaders' expertise at the district level.

2. How do you currently acknowledge and reward the unique contributions of teacher leaders in the school district? Offering teachers opportunities for leadership can be an incentive to assist the district to recruit, retain, and reward accomplished teachers.

For College and University Professors

1. Assess the extent to which your preservice teachers are being prepared to interact productively and communicate effectively with those who are different from them. Given the diversity your graduates will encounter in the future, how can your courses and programs place more emphasis in this area?

2. Recent literature touts teacher research as a new form of teacher leadership that has the potential to influence schoolwide improvement efforts. As a faculty, reflect on ways in which preservice teachers can be engaged in learning about and performing inquiry projects. Further consider how the findings of these research efforts can be used to influence your graduates' classroom practices.

7

Emerging Teacher Leadership and Its Challenges

It means I'm no longer "just a teacher." I am surprised and humbled to discover that I have become a teacher leader and have the opportunity to be a contributing member of the education profession if I'm willing to accept the challenge. It requires I be informed. It requires I keep an open mind and a respectful demeanor. It requires that I assume good intentions and live with compromise. It requires I never neglect my students in order to serve my profession.

Susan Graham, Family and Consumer
Science Teacher Leader

After almost 20 years of working with teacher leaders, we are encouraged that they are emerging as legitimate contributors, who are moving beyond traditional classroom responsibilities. We are inspired by the way teachers, in spite of many obstacles, are taking on leadership that is more complex than occasional involvement in school improvement. Recognizing the value of tapping into these outstanding teachers, many school systems are establishing policies, designing professional development, and supporting teacher leaders in order to take advantage of these resources. Along with these expanded opportunities to lead and influence, the teachers themselves face numerous predictable and unique challenges.

Evolution of Teacher Leadership

Teacher leader roles have evolved from highly individualized roles, such as those of department chairpersons, to instructional leadership roles in which teacher leaders attempt to engage all teachers in the improvement of teaching and learning. In the 1980s, teacher leadership was exhibited by teachers in positions such as those of department chairperson and team leader, who were expected to have expertise in their subject matter or grade level. Then in the early 1990s, the focus of improvement changed to include whole-school reform through shared decision making. Teachers became involved in the governance of schools. Later in that decade, standards-based reform was mandated, and schools were encouraged to work toward building professional learning communities. Collective teacher leadership emerged in the few schools that were able to actually build community. Presently, the press of accountability has led to numerous teacher leader roles in school-based instructional leadership. Table 7.1 illustrates the evolution of teacher leader roles.

We believe that all teachers can select appropriate leadership roles for themselves, given their own experience, confidence level, skills,

Table 7.1   Evolution of Teacher Leadership From 1980 to the Present

1980s	Department Chairperson/Team Leader	Subject Matter/Grade-Level Expertise
Early to Mid 1990s	Governance Leadership	Whole-School Reform Shared Decision Making
Mid to Late 1990s	Collective Teacher Leadership	Standards-Based Reform Professional Learning Communities
2000s	School-Based Instructional Leadership	Accountability

and knowledge. The teacher leader role may be informal or formal and may last only a short time or be a long-term commitment. The vast number of teacher leader roles precludes specific descriptions of all teacher leader roles. These roles emerge within a school or district context that determines the function of the role and the tasks assumed by these teacher leaders. The goal is to find the best *fit* between the task and the teacher leader. The variety of roles and responsibilities increases as schools and school systems recognize how valuable teacher leadership can be in addressing improved student learning. In addition, as the concept of teacher leadership is better understood by teachers and the impact of teacher leadership acknowledged, there may be less reluctance to take on leadership.

Many Faces of Teacher Leadership

Informal teacher leadership permeates a school. The variety in types of informal teacher leader roles is endless and often depends on the interests of the teachers and the needs of the particular school. These are the teacher leaders who make a difference through "careful, thoughtful, small, practical efforts . . . working far from the limelight" (Badaracco, 2002, p. 9). In an ideal school setting, all teachers assume varying levels of leadership within a community of professional learners. In the real world of education, though, effective school administrators do not rely on volunteerism and invite many teachers to accept both informal and formal roles. The school and district context determines the type and level of teacher leadership involvement.

Teacher leaders in formal roles include instructional coaches, lead teachers, mentors, staff developers, data analysts, and others, and they may be

Focused on the classroom, the school, or the school district.

Closely related to a specific discipline, or defined as generalists.

Individual contributors, or involved in group or team interactions.

In highly formalized roles, or simply one-time contributors.

Chosen by election of peers, by appointment through administrators, or by self-selection.

Teacher leadership roles appear to separate into four leadership functions. First, teacher leaders may function in governance capacities within or outside the school. Second, a teacher leader may offer leadership to support student activities. Third, the function of a teacher leader may be to contribute to operational tasks within or outside the school. Finally, teacher leaders may take on instructional leadership responsibilities. Many teacher leaders cross over the lines of these functions and accept multiple tasks.

Leadership in Governing

Teachers are immersed in school decision making through membership on school improvement teams, school advisory councils, or steering committees. Teachers also act as leaders through their partnerships with parents, businesses, and community members in formally and informally structured organizations. Educational foundations, parent-teacher organizations, and community action groups are all examples of the types of organizations in which teachers work with outside stakeholders. Chairing committees on such issues as textbook selection, school redistricting, or teacher evaluation are other examples of teacher leadership functions in which teachers influence both policy and practice. Within schools, teacher leaders serve as faculty chairpersons or parent-teacher organization officers or take other elected positions within the governance structure.

Leadership of Student Activities

Student-oriented leadership roles may involve teachers in coordinating academic programs that extend beyond the regular curriculum, such as Odyssey of the Mind competitions. Teachers may be involved in conceptualizing and carrying out programs based on student academic needs, such as mentoring programs involving retirees or business people working with underachieving students or afterschool tutoring activities conducted by older students for younger students. In our experience, teachers often recognize other needs of students and create strategies to meet these needs, such as Fitness Clubs to focus on student health concerns or music, dance, or theater groups to allow students to express themselves through the arts.

Leadership in Operational Tasks

Operational tasks keep the school organized and moving toward its goals. Teacher leaders serve in formal roles such as department or grade-level chairperson, team leader, and faculty council or staff development chairperson (Gabriel, 2005). Other leadership activities may involve teachers as action researchers working in collaboration with a local university. Some teachers take on more formal leadership roles in their professional organizations. Teachers serve on task forces, boards, and commissions that have a voice in the design of state or district curriculum and assessment or assist local universities with curriculum reform efforts in teacher education programs. Additional functions might include teacher leaders as grant writers, project managers, or technology experts. Applying for school accreditation engages teacher leaders in active roles of preparing their schools for the process or serving on visiting teams for other schools.

Leadership in Instruction

Teachers assume leadership roles with students in the classroom, such as facilitator, coach, provider of feedback, and counselor. Beyond the classroom, teacher leaders serve as mentors, coaches, teacher trainers, curriculum specialists, or simply as willing listeners. Teacher leaders can provide critically needed support to beginning teachers, to those who are teaching a different subject area, or to experienced teachers who are new to the school (Lieberman & Miller, 2004). Teacher leaders can serve as coaches of other teachers and observers of their instructional practice. They also lead by creating new and innovative approaches with students, such as student-led conferencing or ongoing mentoring. Teachers lead collegial study groups or invite colleagues to observe their lessons. Exchanging materials with other teachers or planning with an interdisciplinary team the best way to help an individual student to be successful are other examples of leadership. Teachers may also serve as mentors to others who are seeking certification from the National Board for Professional Teaching Standards (NBPTS).

Within the roles of instructional teacher leader, three types of positions have evolved. The first type is developed to address a pressing need in a school, such as coordinating a mentoring program for non-certificated teachers entering the profession as a second career. M. Donaldson et al. (2008) described individuals in these positions as "non-reform" teacher leaders. These teacher leaders may address areas of school reform, but they are not charged with changing teacher practice. Teacher leaders in these roles are perceived as non-threatening by other teachers in the school.

The second type of teacher leader position is focused on teaching and learning practices and challenges the teacher leader to work with other teachers regarding their work with students in order to improve student achievement. M. Donaldson et al. (2008) identify these positions as "reform roles" (p. 3). The teacher leader reform roles became prominent in response to evident gaps in the achievement of students, particularly in those areas that are tested, such as reading, writing, and mathematics. The impetus for the proliferation of these positions was not on how to provide teachers with career options; instead, it was to address the politically charged pressure to improve student achievement, especially on standardized tests. Teacher leaders serving as literacy coaches, professional developers, and curriculum coordinators are but a few of the individuals who fall into this category. These teacher leaders move outside the classroom to provide support for other teachers who are striving or are identified as needing to improve their instruction. The expectation is that teacher leaders will work closely with other teachers to address teaching practices. They may work within a single school or work with several schools, but their role and responsibilities are determined by leaders within the specific school or school system.

Finally, the third type of teacher leadership surfaces when teachers work together collaboratively within a professional learning community. The teacher leaders either do not leave the classroom or continue to teach some classes, while they collaborate with teachers to learn from their students' work to improve instruction. This teacher leadership focuses on solving arising problems in instruction, student life, or other areas of concern. A temporary role, this kind of leadership may move from teacher to teacher depending on a teacher's interest, changes in teacher assignments, or other extenuating factors. If a school culture is supportive and collaborative, this type of leadership can be a powerful source for change.

It is tempting to advocate solely for teacher leadership that occurs within a professional learning community. If every school had healthy working conditions, a faculty of outstanding teachers, and resources to support initiatives, then this would be the most logical approach to teacher leadership. In the real world, schools are functioning along a continuum from an ideal school culture to dysfunctional working conditions where few teachers are competent, credible, and approachable. School leaders charged with the responsibility for ensuring quality education for all students must make the decision as to the type of teacher leadership needed within a school. This decision is situational; it depends on the working conditions, the quality of teaching, and the student outcomes.

Since schools are unique, differentiated approaches to leadership must be developed. Teacher leaders may be willing take initiative, but they must be realistic regarding the challenges they will face on their leadership journey. We identify these challenges and suggest what teacher leaders and others can do to deliberately ensure that their leadership makes a difference.

Challenges for Teacher Leaders

Moving from the security of the classroom into collaboration with administrators, teachers, and others is risky for many reasons. Teacher leaders who have stepped up and intend to accept these roles should recognize the complexity of their involvement before they agree to take on these roles. Although these challenges may be common to all types of teacher leadership, these are especially crucial for instructional teacher leadership roles. How teachers address the issues depends on their specific roles and responsibilities. In this section we explore four challenges:

Deciding to accept a leadership role

Building principal/teacher leader relationships

Working with peers

Facilitating professional learning for self and others

Deciding to Accept a Leadership Role

Although teachers may be intrigued by the lure of moving into a leadership role, there are areas to consider before applying for a position or agreeing to assume these responsibilities. Impacting the decision will be the relationships that exist within the context in which the teacher leader will work. The four areas for the potential teacher leader to assess include administrative support, the teaching culture, history of professional learning, and personal balance.

First, it is important to understand to what extent the school district and school leaders are committed to sharing leadership with teachers. If principals are open to sharing power and authority, it will be easier for teacher leaders to move forward to lead on their own initiative. On the other hand, if the principal espouses support of the teacher leadership role and then undermines it or is not accessible to partner with the teacher leader, one can predict difficulties. In other situations, the principal may be supportive but is offered little flexibility from the central office leaders, who do not promote teacher leadership and put up obstacles in accessing resources. In these kinds of situations, the teacher leader will have challenges.

Perhaps the most important concern for teacher leaders is working with other teachers, who may perceive the teacher leader's role as threatening or, at the least, not meaningful. The degree of collegiality, as measured by the Teacher Leader School Survey (TLSS) (see Resource B), should be considered and may include reflection on questions such as, do teachers discuss strategies and share materials? Or, do teachers in my school observe one another's work with students? In many school cultures, teacher leaders face barriers that are too difficult to hurdle regardless of the competence, hard work, or persistence of the teacher leader. This type of culture pushes teacher leaders toward burnout and often convinces them that they need to stay in the classroom where it is safe. Taking time to assess the teaching culture is important, even if the teacher leader will be working in the school where she currently teaches.

Next, an examination of the history of professional learning in the school and school system is critical. Teacher leadership is about professional growth, and it is crucial to know if a school has a commitment to ongoing professional learning or a developmental focus as measured by the TLSS. This commitment cannot be determined by a count of how many teachers attended workshops, conferences, or other sometimes fragmented events, but rather, commitment to professional development is measured in terms of the extent to which the student learning needs are assessed and professional development planned based on what teachers need to know and do in order to meet those needs. Do the school administrators and teacher leaders claim to work in a professional learning community but then attempt to work in a setting in which no time, structures, or resources for this collaboration are provided? Without support, it will be difficult for a teacher leader to promote professional learning.

Finally, teachers should look at their personal needs. To take on teacher leadership is enticing, possibly ego satisfying, but if the result is a lack of balance in one's life, then there will be disappointment and disillusionment. Reflecting on the advantages and disadvantages of assuming a teacher leader role may be time saving in the long run. Although we encourage teachers to contribute as leaders, we are aware that this level of involvement is not for every teacher. Also, there are times in a teacher's career when it is wise to move in and out of leadership roles based on the context of the work and the level of outside commitments and obligations in one's personal life. Table 7.2 summarizes these factors.

Table 7.2 Factors Influencing Success as a Teacher Leader

Organizational Commitment to Teacher Leadership	Teaching Culture
• Does the principal understand the value of and support teacher leaders? • Will I have resources and time to perform my leadership role? • What is the extent of my authority in accessing both human and fiscal resources? • What evidence is there of informal teacher leadership? • How do teachers interact with existing teacher leaders in the school? • Are teachers encouraged to authentically participate and give input to critical decisions?	• Are the teachers open to working with me? • Are the teachers entrenched in their practice, or do they frequently seek professional learning? • What are the relationships between and among teachers? • How do those who all teach within the same content area, or who have different levels of teaching experience, interact? • Are the social networks in the school healthy or dysfunctional? • Is time allocated for teachers to work together? Are they expected to work together on instructional issues?
Professional Learning	**Personal Balance**
• Are teachers accustomed to being observed and observing other teachers? • Do teachers currently collaborate with each other to improve teaching and learning? • What is the history of reform initiatives and professional learning in the school? • Is there a functioning professional learning community? Or is professional learning not taken seriously?	• Do I have knowledge and skills to effectively teach my subject/grade level? • What is my history of working collaboratively with other teachers? • Have teachers in the past come to me for help in their teaching practice? • Do I have the commitment of family and friends to support me in taking on this role? • What personal obligations do I have that might be neglected?

Teacher leaders are wise to consider the implications of moving into a leadership role, especially if they work in an unhealthy school culture. To carefully assess the context in which the leadership takes place will help a prospective teacher leader know if taking on leadership is the right decision. One strategy is to assess the dimensions of support for teacher leadership evident in the school by completing the TLSS (see Resource B). Once a decision is made, the first step is to build a positive relationship with the principal and other key leaders in the school.

Building Principal–Teacher Relationships

The relationship between the principal and teacher leader is crucial for the teacher leader. If the principal values teacher leadership and is skilled in supporting teacher leadership, then the way is cleared to do meaningful work. Often, though, principals are unaware of their responsibilities toward teacher leaders. With the myriad of external and internal demands on principals, they may not understand how teacher leadership can enhance their work and actually lead to improvement in teaching and learning. School districts may allocate funds for teacher leaders, such as literacy coaches, while not recognizing the need to prepare the principals, who may misunderstand the purpose of the position, resent the imposition of a new responsibility, or be unskilled in working with the teacher leader. Teacher leaders need to take responsibility for building the relationship with the principal and initiate discussions for reaching mutual agreements on the teacher leaders' roles and boundaries.

The word *power* is often rejected by teachers because of the association with authoritarian models of leadership. Leadership, though, is best when leaders use what resources, or power, they have to make a difference in the lives of others. Both principals and teachers have power. Principals have positional power and as a result are expected to respond to the expectations of the school system. Meanwhile, teacher leaders may have personal power through their relationships with teachers and others in the school community. Recognizing that each can gain from contributing to the other person's success, it can become evident that both the principal and the teacher leader can benefit if they work collaboratively. To work together effectively, principals and teacher leaders must share their power or their resources.

Without a clear agreement on how the principal and teacher will work together, there can be numerous misunderstandings. Principals, with the best intentions, may give the teacher leader autonomy to work without negotiating roles and responsibilities. Under pressure to solve school problems, principals sometimes ask teacher leaders to take on administrative duties that pull them away from working with students and teachers. In the busy world of schools, time can go by without conversations between the principal and the teacher regarding action steps and expected outcomes. As teacher leaders begin their work, they often take initiative and make decisions that principals feel are not the teacher's responsibility. Finally, teacher leaders are caught in the middle between the principal and other staff members; therefore, they may not be able to access resources, because the staff is not informed about the teacher leaders' roles. All these challenges can result in wasted time, frustration, and a damaged principal–teacher leader relationship.

A practical approach to this challenge is to negotiate the principal–teacher leader working relationship. Communication using the FLEX listening skills (see Chapter 6) and the ADS model (see Chapter 4) is essential to the success of this negotiation. Prior to the conversation, it is best for the teacher leader to list areas in which agreement needs to be reached. In addition, the teacher leader could request that the principal make a similar list. Listed below are possible areas of negotiation. An informal teacher leader would not be interested in discussing many of the items, but full time instructional teacher leaders would consider all these areas as relevant for their work:

- Determining the scope of the teacher leader's roles and responsibilities
- Identifying specific dates and times that the principal and teacher will meet to share information, measure progress, and generate action steps
- Determining the outcomes the teacher leader will be held accountable for within a timetable
- Delineating the areas of decision making for which the teacher is and is not responsible
- Developing a plan for how the principal will communicate to other teachers, staff, and parents the responsibilities of the teacher leader
- Gaining permission and explaining how to access human and fiscal resources within and outside the school
- Establishing approaches for working with external audiences, such as the central office personnel, community leaders, and parents

It would be overwhelming to negotiate all these issues in one meeting. Rather the first meeting should be a time for both the principal and the teacher leader to share their lists of concerns and decide on when and how they will reach agreement. Attention to putting crucial issues on the table will take time, but it will result in building positive principal–teacher leader relationships. Depending on the school culture, teacher leaders must decide how to balance this relationship with their relationships with peers.

Working With Peers

In the current structure of teaching cultures, there is reason for concern on the part of teacher leaders regarding their relationships with other teachers. Most teachers know of or have experienced the hurt of stepping outside the norm of a serving as a classroom teacher and meeting with resistance from colleagues, even those who were considered friends. This may be based on competitive feelings, professional jealousy, or simply lack of experience with the idea that teachers can learn from each other.

Most teacher leaders believe that peer relationships are the biggest challenge. The teaching profession is designed as a flat profession in which every teacher is expected to be equal, except in seniority. Moving outside this norm can be treacherous for teacher leaders, because this violates the norm of equality and implies that the teacher leaders are more expert than other teachers in the school. The teacher leaders are caught in the middle between the administration and their peers. Plus the teacher leader may appear to have access to the principal, a currency coveted by most teachers.

Concern about relationships with others within their schools also becomes an obstacle to a teacher leader's success. When asked to identify barriers, one teacher told us, "I guess the barrier is me." Findings from a recent study concur with this teacher's opinion. Evidence suggests that teachers themselves are a barrier in second-wave reform efforts: "Caught in social norms about teachers' work with students, job redesign may be rejected by teachers themselves" (Smylie & Denny, 1990, p. 257). We believe the time has come to challenge the isolation and the egalitarian norms that exist in many schools. Teachers continue to struggle with concerns about the reactions of peers to their leadership activities. Fears of opposition to their ideas and of being criticized are real to teachers who want to maintain positive relations with their colleagues. Teacher leaders in a recent study reported feeling that other teachers "resent them, their success, and their visibility" (Zinn, 1997, p. 10). It is no wonder that, as we have worked with teachers across the country, there has been reluctance among some to call themselves leaders.

In a study of both "reform teacher leaders," such as literacy coaches, and "non-reform teacher leaders," such as department chairpersons, M. Donaldson et al. (2008) found that the expectation of equality, "seniority," and threats to "autonomy" made it difficult for reform teacher leaders to work with their peers. In fact, teachers resented the identified teacher leaders and resisted collaborating with them. On the other hand, "non-reform" teachers did not have the same resistance from their peers. The reason for this difference was that the reform teachers attempted to step into the instructional domain of their peers, which has always been untouchable in the past. Teachers, who cherish their autonomy, are likely to view their instructional practices as satisfactory and are reluctant to receive feedback from others, especially another teacher. In addition, teachers can become resentful about the recognition and rewards, such as released time, give to teacher leaders. Informal teacher leaders may not face the same level of resentment, but they must learn how to collaborate so that they can influence practice beyond their classrooms.

The teacher leader role is relatively new, and these teachers, who have few opportunities to learn leadership skills, rely on strategies they devise on their own to survive. Unfortunately some teacher leaders diminish their position or deny their authority through applying such strategies. Some teachers reject suggestions and offers of help from the teacher leader. Working with teachers leaders, we find that when we share these strategies, they reluctantly admit they use them. For example, teacher leaders

- Provide materials for teachers, who will expect more and more resources.
- Take on the same duties, for example bus duty, as other teachers and then have to work beyond the school day to complete their teacher leader responsibilities.
- Tell teachers that they are only facilitators and do not have any power.
- Dissociate themselves from administrators, even if there are good relationships between them.
- Give only positive feedback to teachers when they observe.

It is hard to blame teacher leaders for using these techniques to win the favor of other teachers, but they are unable to influence teaching and learning throughout the school, because they only work with the willing teachers. Mangin (2005) found that teachers were not always reluctant to work with teacher leaders when the teacher leader worked within the context of the teacher's classroom, and the assistance was "non-threatening, saved time, provided new information, and facilitated complex instruction . . . with instructional support, such as classroom assistance and model lessons" (p. 47).

The goal of instructional leadership by teachers is to engage with other teachers in professional learning. In order to do this, the teacher leader must be able to effectively access the teachers in their classrooms. Collaboration, dialogue, and other forms of talk outside the classroom are important, but for change to happen, it must be between teachers and their students.

Facilitating the Learning of Self and Others

When we speak with teacher leaders, almost every conversation involves talking about professional learning, whether for themselves or other teachers. Teacher leaders like to learn; in fact, we could say they are passionate about learning. On the other hand, competent teachers usually gain satisfaction from sharing their knowledge with other teachers. The challenge is designing, facilitating, and reinforcing quality professional learning, and teacher leaders need this knowledge in order to effectively lead. One teacher leader said to us recently, "I had no idea what it took to prepare a great instructional design for professional development."

Changes need to be made to ensure that teacher leaders are provided with career-long professional developmental opportunities. Professional development of teacher leaders should be viewed as a continuum of opportunities. Early-career teachers may want to focus on developing their competency as leaders of their students, and then credibility with their colleagues naturally follows. In due course, teacher leaders can develop readiness to reach out to assist their peers and to work on schoolwide leadership efforts. To develop this level of competence, changes in professional development are needed to ensure that teachers have input into their own professional growth and that job-embedded approaches are used to ensure that learning is connected to practice. Professional reading, coaching, study groups, networks, and acceptance of responsibility for assignments delegated by administrators at school are a few of the developmental strategies that could overcome the separation of learning and classroom practice. Much promise is seen in the movement toward professional learning communities within schools; increased learning and professionalism among all teachers, coupled with collaborative environments, can help to make significant changes in the way our students are taught and in the outcomes we are able to produce.

Professional development, like teacher leadership, has evolved along with the changes in school reform. This parallel development is illustrated in Figure 7.1. Isolated workshops were the venue for training teachers to use the teacher-proof curriculum in the 1970s. Participants in the workshops were not invited to understand how the new curriculum could fit into their existing practice. Instead, the trainer delivered a curriculum package with the expectation that strategies would be used intact. The teachers returned to their classrooms and taught the way they thought was most effective. No one paid attention to the teachers' concerns about the new curriculum, so the teachers continued to teach in ways they believed were best for their students (Hall & Hord, 1987).

Figure 7.1   Parallel Evolution of School Reform and Professional Development

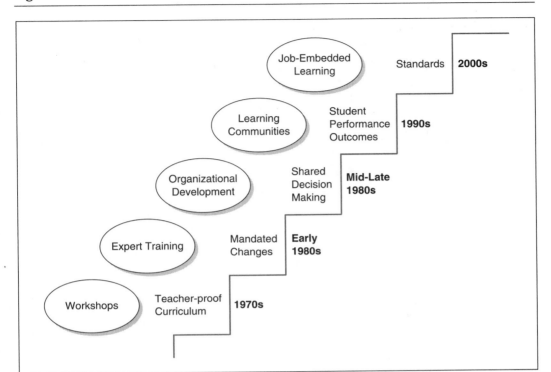

During the 1980s, policymakers, impatient with a lack of progress toward school reform, mandated changes monitored by basic skills testing that stressed selected skills in reading, writing, and mathematics. External trainers, who seldom taught in classrooms, sent a message to teachers that they needed "fixing" and were incapable of creating adequate learning environments for their students. The teachers rarely saw the strategies as relevant to their work.

When the mandated policies did not result in adequate improvement in student performance, the reform movement began to focus on governance issues. As school governance structures changed, teachers were pushed into the formidable task of collaborating with each other. Organizational development interventions, a form of professional development, were designed to diagnose the status of these working relationships and to suggest process strategies for group work. In some situations, this reliance on an outside consultant to rescue and fix the school resulted in deficit models of professional development and did not stimulate all leaders at the school to engage in substantive reform efforts.

If people external to the school could not influence change, then the focus was on the educators in the schools. In the late 1990s professional learning communities were touted as organic structures that engage teachers and other staff in collaborative learning and improve student learning (Louis & Marks, 1996). The complexity of context factors, inadequate leadership skills, and the little time available in schools limited the growth of professional learning communities.

While the professional learning community is still a worthy goal, today we know that unless there is job-embedded professional learning, predictably there will be few changes in teaching and learning. The typical afterschool workshops and pull-out sessions without assessment of student needs, collaborative planning, and monitoring of outcomes is a waste of valuable resources, including teachers' time. Within schools, job-embedded learning is enhanced through individualized professional development plans. The growth in individualized professional development has been influenced by the growing number of teachers who are NBPTS certified.

Teachers recognize these problems with professional learning and lament that most school systems still rely on fragmented workshops. No wonder teachers are reluctant to participate in professional development; they doubt they can benefit from taking time away from their classrooms or their personal lives for a repeat of these experiences. Understanding the need for quality professional learning and the gap between the current situation and the ideal is the first step for teacher leaders who wish to make a difference in their schools.

For teachers who enjoy their own professional learning, it can be rewarding to explore the field of professional learning so that they can influence instructional practice in their schools and school districts. Here are strategies to move in this direction:

- Join a professional organization that focuses on professional learning, such as the National Staff Development Council (www.nsdc.org). Read the publications, visit the Web site, and attend national and state conferences.
- Find a leader who is knowledgeable about professional learning and who is regarded as competent, credible, and approachable. Request to shadow and learn from this person or invite the person to mentor you.
- Read books and journal articles about adult learning, professional development, and school change (see Resource D).

- Request assistance from competent professional developers in the design, facilitation, and follow-up of professional learning.
- Align your professional learning plan with the school's improvement plan.

We believe that teacher leaders are part of a community of leaders and learners. In order to influence teaching and learning in a school, teacher leaders join with other teachers to continuously learn.

Conclusion

All leaders face challenges, but teacher leaders face obstacles that are unique to existing school cultures, especially instructional teacher leaders. Formal leadership rests with principals, and if the teacher leaders have strong working relationships with them, the work is more productive. The flat teaching profession sets expectations that every teacher will be treated the same regardless of the teacher's competence, and the identification of a teacher leader in the school setting challenges that belief. Teacher leaders must take the initiative to address these challenges. Waiting for other people, such as the principal or school district leaders, to solve them may be futile. Teacher leaders can take steps to be proactive and make a difference in their schools.

We are at the beginning of a new era in teacher leadership. The obstacles we described in this chapter are to be expected as this new type of leadership emerges. These issues may always exist, but as the future of teacher leadership unfolds, there will be more recognition for the value of involving teachers in authentic leadership.

APPLICATION CHALLENGES

For Teachers

1. After reading the challenges for teacher leaders in this chapter, identify the challenges you face as a teacher engaged in leadership activities. Are they the same or different? Find support and problem solving assistance through face-to-face or electronic networking with other teacher leaders.

2. Explore the context in your school for the possibility and promise of authentic teacher leadership work. Respond to the Teacher Leadership School Survey (see Resource B) and assess your

school. Discuss your perceptions with others in your building. Identify areas of strength and areas to be developed in supporting teacher leadership in your school.

For Principals and Assistant Principals

1. Administrators' actions can serve either as supporting or hindering forces to a teacher leader's work. Identify how you can intensify the supporting forces, for example, by providing effective leadership training for teacher leaders or by finding time for regular meetings with teacher leaders. Likewise, identify ways to overcome barriers and obstacles that are hindering teacher leaders. Examples might include thoughtful consideration of how to communicate the role of teacher leaders to the whole faculty or how you might involve teachers in the selection of teachers for leadership roles.

2. Structures in the school influence the success of teacher leaders in impacting teaching and learning. Initiate dialogue with teacher leaders about structures such as job descriptions for their work, team and grade-level arrangements for scheduling common planning time, grouping of students into classrooms, and space for meetings and collaborative work.

For Superintendents and District Staff

1. As formal "reform-focused" teacher leadership roles are introduced, consider how to balance expectations for the work of these leaders between promoting district mandates and priorities and responding to school-level needs. As district staff, consider how you will best assure accountability while maintaining appropriate autonomy for teacher leaders.

2. Sophisticated skills are required of teachers who take on instructional leadership roles, and expectations for these positions have increased in the accountability era. How will your district most effectively select, develop, assign, and offer long-term support to these teachers? How will your district evaluate the extent to which these teacher leaders are able to influence instructional practice at your school sites?

For College and University Professors

1. University coursework prepares teachers with subject area/content knowledge that is applied in their own classrooms. As teachers take on

more leadership roles in the future and attempt to influence instruction beyond their own classrooms, what needs to be added to their preparation programs to enable them to foster instructional improvement on a school wide basis?

2. Substantive research to inform the development and implementation of emerging roles for teacher leaders is needed. Answers to questions about the impact of instructional teacher leadership roles on school improvement, on instructional practices, and finally on linkages of teacher leadership to student outcomes are needed. How can higher education assist schools and districts in this regard?

8

Building a Future for Teacher Leadership

Part of the dilemma facing school districts that find themselves confronting previously unimagined challenges is not only learning how to use teachers as part of the leadership team that transforms our schools, but knowing with at least a limited degree of certainty what they are getting with "teacher leaders," particularly if funding for these positions is to ever become sustainable.

Andrew Davis, English Teacher Leader

Teacher leaders work long hours, endure challenging peer relationships, and attempt to balance their professional and personal lives. With these demands, we would expect that these talented educators would question what the future holds for them. Many say they can persevere if they know that there are efforts being made to improve the working conditions for them. The future for teacher leadership is promising; it holds possibilities that will engage teachers as legitimate leaders within their schools and the larger educational community. Although many of the ideas are only seeds of innovation, they are being spread throughout the professional literature, policy discussions, and pilot programs to test how teacher leaders can be supported.

Teacher leadership is no longer a concept that is unfamiliar to most educators. School reform initiatives, concern about literacy, and accountability demands have influenced schools and school districts to look at the resources within their systems, especially accomplished teachers. Another contributing factor to the increased interest in teacher leadership is the initiative shown by a critical mass of teachers certified by the National Board for Professional Teaching Standards (NBPTS) who are examining their profession and volunteering to help other teachers engage in improving their craft.

In the early 1990s, when we wrote the first edition of this book, few people understood the concept of teacher leadership. Principals and other formal leaders would hesitate when we asked them to identify teacher leaders in their schools. Teachers were especially leery of our questions about their "leadership." In fact, the title of this book—*Awakening the Sleeping Giant*—was influenced by a response of one of the most gifted teacher leaders we know. When we asked about her leadership, she said: "Oh, no! I'm not a leader. The teacher union reps are leaders, but not me." This teacher had just left a meeting with the superintendent of her school system during which she had influenced him to allow her to establish study groups across the school district. If this isn't leadership, what is?

Recent reviews of the research literature (Mangin & Stoelinga, 2008; York-Barr & Duke, 2004) reveal that it has been only in the last 20 years that our field has acknowledged this type of leadership, and even today there are few empirical studies that examine teacher leadership. The vast literature regarding school leadership spans many decades, but most is focused on the principal. If we are to better understand teacher leadership, then we must engage those from schools, school systems, and universities to grapple with overcoming the constraints and providing the support systems teacher leaders need in their workplaces. Further inquiry is warranted to uncover the true benefits of teachers' providing leadership within and beyond their classrooms, influencing others toward improved educational practice, participating as learners and leaders in community with their peers, and taking responsibility for their leadership. The insights that could be gained from research can inform the practice of school leaders and the preparation of teachers and will contribute to the bottom line—outcomes for students.

The good news is that teacher leadership is being studied and promoted in numerous schools and school systems, and it is emerging as a viable resource for improving teaching and learning. The challenging news is that there is much work to be done in order to fully take advantage of these resources. Despite teacher leadership becoming more widely recognized, many schools and districts still do not understand, are hesitant to promote, or are not committed to teacher leadership. The schools in which teacher leadership is accepted as a norm are multiplying, but we have not yet arrived at a point at which it is accepted throughout our profession. Why is teacher leadership not thriving in all of the schools across our country today? What will it take to make teacher leadership an acknowledged resource? What needs to change in terms of norms, organizational structures, policy and practice, and use of resources to pave the way for teacher leadership?

Based on our discussions with teacher leaders and our experience in their development as leaders, there are recurring themes. Some constraints are from the teacher leaders themselves; others are woven into the context in which they do their work. In this chapter, first we look at predictions regarding the future of teacher leadership by considering what might be in place to fully take advantage of it. Then we examine three areas of concern—career opportunities, working conditions, and compensation—that must be addressed in order to realize the full potential of teacher leadership. In previous chapters, we suggested application challenges for various stakeholders, but in this chapter we focus on how teacher leaders can learn advocacy skills in order to take initiatives that may result in a powerful future for teacher leadership. Perhaps no other group can better influence the community and the general public than high-quality and respected teachers. These are the people who face the day-to-day challenges that are affected by public opinion and policy decisions.

Teacher Leadership in the Future

The new generations of teachers, retention of teachers, and the need to significantly improve learning for all students provide the impetus to influence the future of teacher leadership. What will teacher leadership look like 10 or 20 years from now? If the giant, untapped resource of teacher leadership is to serve the schools, the incremental evolution of school reform as we know it must be accelerated. Small changes will no longer be enough; reinvention is needed. Over eight years ago the Institute for Educational Leadership (2001) stated the issue succinctly:

> It is not too late for education's policymakers to exploit a potentially splendid resource for leadership and reform that is now being squandered: the experience, ideas, and capacity to lead of the nation's schoolteachers. (p. 2)

The resource of teacher leadership is perhaps recognized by a broader group of educators and policymakers now than it has been in the past, but it will take significant changes to prevent these talents from being squandered in the future. Next we describe how the future of teacher leadership might look.

Rather than being a rare phenomenon in public schools, teacher leadership will grow to be an organizational expectation. The role of teacher leader will be motivating and challenging in the schools of the future. Teachers will accept empowerment as their right rather than shy away from leadership because of experiences with pseudo-involvement in decision making. Teachers and other stakeholders will enjoy mutually satisfying relationships working together on the common goal of improving education for all students. No longer will there be the selected few teacher leaders, who previously faced the disdain of their colleagues; instead, all teachers will be invited to participate in a community of leaders, with teachers taking on additional roles based on their competence, interest, and personal circumstances.

Teachers will not be expected to take on leadership roles without support from the school systems, including salary compensation. District leaders, who recognize their roles as serving schools and teachers, will engage teachers as legitimate partners in substantive decision making. While principals and other formal leaders in a school system participate in professional learning to enhance their leadership, teacher leaders will be colearners, because important features of the production of sustainable outcomes in schools are the activities in which principals, teachers, and other key stakeholders "participate together as mutual learners and leaders" (Lambert, 2002, p. 38) to develop their leadership capacity. Teacher leaders will be given time and resources in order to mentor potential and new teacher leaders in an effort to build leadership capacity throughout the system. NBPTS-certified teachers and other gifted teachers will be recognized and encouraged to take on leadership roles. States, along with school systems, will offer teacher career ladders that are predictable, ongoing, and fully funded. The teachers of the future will expect opportunities to move in and out of leadership roles depending on their personal needs. This flexibility will encourage talented teachers to stay in a profession that is sensitive to expectations of a new generation of teachers.

The impact of working conditions on student learning will be accepted and will be measured, publicly communicated, and addressed with as much fervor as student achievement. As differentiated roles for teacher leaders are planned, the school system and school leaders will work to prepare the teaching culture for acceptance of these roles. Principals, especially, will recognize the value of tapping into teacher leadership, learn how to collaborate with these colleagues, and strive to build a school culture that accepts and rewards teacher leaders. The egalitarian teaching culture will move toward a teaching culture that acknowledges differing levels of leadership participation.

Salaries for teachers will be determined through performance appraisals based on multiple criteria and evaluation by several people. This comprehensive approach to performance evaluation will inform professional learning plans for each teacher based on his or her particular needs and interests in growth and development. Compensation for high-quality teachers will allow teachers to focus on their profession, rather than assuming supplemental jobs to financially survive.

Schools will be restructured through a reallocation of resources so that time will be available for all teachers, as it is for most professionals, for planning and collaborating. Teacher leaders will remain close to the classroom but will have significant time to mentor other teachers, model instructional strategies, and build their own knowledge and skills. School leaders will plan meetings and other events to be efficient and effective in order to honor the teachers' time. Time-saving resources— such as easily accessible office equipment, clerical support, videoconferencing, and online communication—will be commonplace.

Laments like "they'll never let us do it that way," common responses heard from teachers today, will change to "they are us" in schools of the future. Teachers will join with policymakers, parents, and others in the community to increase the effectiveness of schools. Advocacy skills will be an expectation for teacher leaders. Rather than denying teachers access to the public, school systems will encourage teachers to advocate for students.

Besides creating collaborative cultures, teacher leaders will be called upon to develop expertise in marketing their schools and in resource development to supplement shrinking state and federal education dollars. Privatized services, such as food service and transportation, will require teacher leaders to be consumers of the materials and services needed to accomplish educational plans developed in cooperation with parents and students.

Teacher unions and associations recognizing the power of teacher leadership in influencing teaching and learning will extend their efforts in these areas in the future. Long supportive of developing teachers as leaders in influencing salary, career ladders, working conditions, and specific other areas of policy and practice, these organizations will, in the future, simultaneously work toward developing the capacity of their members to influence student outcomes. Organizations such as the American Federation of Teachers, the National Education Association, and the Coalition of Independent Educators will continue to advance the cause of teacher leadership. By focusing more of their attention and resources on preparing their members to apply instructional research in their classrooms, by offering professional development opportunities for their members, and by championing the significant role of teachers in student success, these organizations will join other stakeholders in reinventing the profession.

A new national, professional organization will be established to serve the needs and interests of teacher leaders. Recognizing the value of external networking, teacher leaders will move beyond their content-specific professional organizations to join together as a force to influence policymakers; national, state, and local school leaders; and other teachers. Frequent opportunities to communicate and learn from one another's experiences will be vital to the teacher leaders.

Finally, teachers will enter the university's teacher preparation programs knowing that they are learning not only about their subject area and pedagogy but also how to be leaders. Those responsible for the preparation of teachers will spend a majority of their time in real school settings. University professors—on site in the schools—and teacher leaders will collaborate to provide the best experiences for preservice teachers. Preparation of educational leaders will place potential teacher leaders, principals, and district staff persons together to learn about leadership.

The role of the university will be to provide opportunities for the students to reflect on their school-site experience, to draw on research and theory to guide their practice, and to help students in assessing their own progress. The question of how schools and universities can learn to work together will be irrelevant; the universities will not participate in teacher or leadership preparation without collaborative relationships with schools. The seeds of revolution in the university's role in schools are being sown now by the leaders in the professional development school movement across the country.

The use of technology and distance learning capabilities will be commonplace and allow preservice and practicing teachers to access universities without traditionally defined borders and campus settings. State-of-the-art learning experiences will cover topics such as cognitive research, group process, human motivation, critical and analytical thinking, media and technology, leadership, and problem solving. A required sequence of coursework for undergraduate and graduate programs will be replaced by a set of expected behaviors, attitudes, and experiences teachers must develop to be prepared for leadership. To strengthen the integration of curriculum, there will be less emphasis on specialization in subject areas and more importance placed on teachers as well-grounded generalists. Teachers will be lifelong learners, and they will supplement their personal knowledge by constantly accessing online databases, as will their students. Many people may enter teaching as one of several careers in a lifetime, and the university will encourage these teachers to capitalize on previous work experiences in preparation for teaching. The separate preparation of future principals and teacher leaders will be replaced with colearning models, so both will understand how to work cooperatively in schools.

So, where do we begin to meet these teacher leadership challenges? We must look at the entire system to make the revolutionary changes; all parts of the system affect the results we can expect. Transformation must extend from the way universities prepare teachers, to the organizational structures of schools today, to the ways we develop and support teacher leaders throughout their careers. Administrative roles will yield to a set of leadership functions accepted by a variety of leaders in the school. The impact of technology, changing demographics, and societal trends give us no choice but to make these changes or risk making an inadequate response to the challenges we will face.

As overwhelming as these systemic changes seem, teacher leaders can work to address those concerns that are closest to their work, such as career opportunities, working conditions, and compensation. Teacher leaders are already working to promote a stronger profession through networks, such as the Teacher Leaders Network (www.teacherleaders.org), and in their personal contacts with policymakers.

Teacher Leader Concerns

In our discussions with teacher leaders, there are three questions they often ask: (1) How will I find ongoing challenges in my career? (2) How can my school be a better workplace? (3) Why am I paid the same as a mediocre teacher? The future of teacher leadership depends on the answers to these questions. To tackle the needs of existing and future teacher leaders, we examine these three key areas. Although there are other critical issues to address, these appear to be the most important to most teacher leaders. Each area is complex and confronts long-held beliefs of both educators and the public.

Expanding Career Opportunities

Changes in school culture norms that allow for teachers to take on formal leadership roles, and yet remain connected to teaching and learning, are essential to the improvement of instructional knowledge and skills. Career ladders, mentoring programs, and other formal approaches place teacher leaders in positions of influence. We have always believed that ultimately, teacher leadership should be for every teacher and should involve teachers in both formal and informal roles. Yet, the "flat-role" expectations for all teachers is part of a myth that suggests all teachers are equally competent, and the contributions of an inexperienced or ineffective teacher is the same as an experienced, effective teacher. We have come to understand, however, that role differentiation in terms of responsibilities and pay can hasten the movement of teachers into roles in which they can support their colleagues to affect student outcomes. Role differentiation may, but it need not, remove teachers from the classrooms where they work with students.

In spite of the need for career options, there are educators who are reluctant to fully embrace a multitiered profession. Their views reflect the history of the teaching culture and constrain efforts to make teaching a true profession. Regardless of the organization, whether in the private sector, the nonprofit sector, or even in a family, the source of power determines where resources reside. Historically, once school administrators entered the scene, teachers withdrew from the leadership roles to their classrooms, where they enjoyed the autonomy of teaching with little or no interference and little power. The quality of teaching depended on the knowledge, skills, and initiative of the individual teacher. It is no secret that not every teacher is competent. We need only observe parents who are actively involved in their children's education, and the distinction between teachers is evidenced by their request or demand to have their children placed in certain teachers' classrooms. The quality of the education for those children who do not have parents as advocates is most often determined by chance.

The press of accountability has pushed schools and school systems to rethink the structure of the teaching profession and salary plans that compensate for the additional knowledge, skills, and responsibilities. Many school systems have already established formal instructional leader roles, such as literacy coach or professional developer. Presently, these teacher leaders, who take on additional responsibilities, usually receive a salary stipend for assuming these roles.

Three examples of models for differentiated teacher leader roles show how the additional responsibilities could be delineated. First, a report from TeacherSolutions (Center for Teaching Quality, 2007) recommends three career levels: novice, advanced, and expert (p. 15). Recognizing that leadership is only one of the factors in a career framework, this group identified the following factors: (1) student learning, (2) knowledge and skills, (3) market needs, and (4) leadership (Table 8.1).

A second real-life example is the Teacher Advancement Program™ (TAP) that is operated in 13 states by the National Institute for Excellence in Teaching. Beginning in 1999, TAP implemented a career continuum (Multiple Career Paths) to include three levels: master teacher, mentor teacher, and career teacher, with salary increments between $2,000 and $11,000 (Teacher Advancement Program Foundation, 2005). Table 8.2 describes the different responsibilities at each of these levels.

Finally, Troen and Boles (2003) depict fictional schools in their book that addresses the problems found within elementary education. In their model, "[a] Millennium School offers teachers a multilevel career path that rewards advanced training and experience with higher levels of pay, responsibility, supervision, and team management" (p. 142). The six teaching positions in their model range from an instructional aide to a chief instructor (Table 8.3).

Even now, teachers have more options for leadership than becoming traditional school administrators. States and school systems are beginning to tap into the instructional leadership of teachers, but although these organizations can benefit from the talents of teacher leaders, they have obligations to build support that sustains teacher leadership. Although working in an individual classroom is rewarding, teacher leaders report that when they are placed in teacher leader roles, it affords them opportunities for challenge,

Table 8.1 Multiple Career Paths: Professional Compensation Framework

Base Salary Range *Negotiable based on credentials, experience, performance*	Career Salary Supplements				Base and Career Pay
	Student Learning	*Knowledge and Skills*	*Market Needs*	*Leadership*	
Novice (year 1–4) **$30,000–$45,000**	**Up to 5%** Individual with evidence of impact	**Up to 5%** Research-based professional development based on induction program improvements in teaching and assessment	**Up to $5,000** for teaching in high-needs schools, subjects, and assignments (Teachers need to demonstrate potential in specific context)	Not ready for role and reward	Can earn **up to** **$55,000**
Advanced (year 5–10) **$46,000–55,000**	**Up to 10%** With evidence of impact beyond own classroom; plus $2,000–$3,500 bonus for building and using new assessments	**Up to 10%** National board certification can earn stipend; research-based professional development; mentoring new teachers; plus demonstrations of how professional development improves student learning	**Up to $10,000** for teaching in high-needs schools, subjects, etc. (Teachers need to demonstrate potential and effectiveness in specific context.)	**Up to 10%** for coaching and mentoring; supporting community development	Can earn **up to** **$85,000**

| Expert (year 10+) | $56,000–$70,000 | Up to 15% With higher rewards for using test scores and other measures to improve student learning beyond own classroom and demonstrate how own skills help other teachers enhance student learning; plus $2,000–$3,500 bonus for building and using new assessments | Up to 15% Same as advanced teacher but 5% more when evidence of knowledge and skills spread through district and state | Up to $15,000 for teaching in high-needs schools, subjects, etc. (Teachers need to demonstrate potential and effectiveness in specific context) | Up to 15% for coaching and community development; plus $10,000 for state and national leadership in developing new products and informing new policies | Can earn up to $130,000 |

Source: Center for Teaching Quality, 2007.

Table 8.2   Multiple Career Paths: Teacher Advancement Program™ (TAP)

Career Paths	*Responsibilities*
Career Teacher	Classroom teacher; participate in TAP meetings and professional learning; collaborate with other teachers on curriculum, instruction, and assessment; develop yearly portfolio
Mentor Teacher	Member of leadership team; facilitate TAP meetings, analyze student data, demonstrate and team teach lessons, coach and evaluate teachers, participate in professional learning
Master Teacher	Member of leadership team; responsible for TAP in school, share instructional leadership role with principal, analyze student/teacher data, oversee professional growth plans, disseminate research-based instructional strategies, team teach lessons, coach and evaluate teachers, participate in professional learning, facilitate curriculum and assessment planning and evaluation

Source: Adapted from Teacher Advancement Program Foundation, 2005.

Table 8.3   Multilevel Career Path: A Millennium School

Tiers	*Responsibilities*
Teaching Intern	Undergraduate or graduate student; spend full time for at least a year in the classroom
Associate Teacher	Classroom teacher (less than full time); observe other teachers, attend professional learning experiences
Teacher	Full time classroom teacher
Professional Teacher	Classroom teacher; supervise interns, mentor associate teachers, and/or engage in teacher research/curriculum development
Chief Instructor	Team leader; supervise and mentor other teachers, contribute to profession (e.g., publish articles about work), maintain high level of competence

Source: Adapted from Troen and Boles, 2003.

professional growth, and gaining a broader perspective. Still we are a long way from structuring career options that were recommended almost 23 years ago by the Carnegie Forum on Education and the Economy (1986):

Not only do professionals typically have a range of support staff and services available, but they are usually organized so that the most able among them influence in many ways the work that others do, from broad policy direction to the development of staff responsibilities. This . . . is a matter of simple efficiency, making sure that the experience and skill embodied in these valuable people makes itself felt throughout the enterprise. (p. 40, as cited in Berg, 2007, p. 3)

It is obvious that our schools have not embraced the recommendations of this task force. For example, there are over 74,000 teachers who have attained NBPTS certification (National Board for Professional Teaching Standards, 2008a), yet few states, school systems, or schools effectively engage these teachers to influence teaching or educational policies. In fact, there are leaders in schools and school systems that do not even recognize these accomplished teachers who work through the rigorous certification process. In order for the resource of teacher leadership to fully reach its potential, schools and school systems must address the context in which this resource is used.

Teacher leaders are already influencing policymakers about career opportunities for themselves, as evidenced by the model presented by TeacherSolutions (see Table 8.1). These trailblazers are working in a difficult territory and need the support of their fellow teacher leaders. The first step teacher leaders can take is to become informed about the existing efforts to expand career options; the next step is to put their efforts behind those they feel will make a difference. Paralleling career paths, though, must be the development compensation that rewards teacher leaders for their work. Professionals who take on leadership responsibilities should be able to count on reasonable increments in their salaries based on a pay-for-performance model.

Providing Adequate Compensation

The lack of rewards for teacher leadership must also be addressed. Meeting the monetary and nonmonetary needs of teachers profoundly affects the chances of making a difference in teachers' willingness to serve as leaders. A single-salary schedule for teachers has outlived its usefulness. When it was introduced over 90 years ago, there were good reasons for a uniform compensation plan, such as gender bias and racial inequities that resulted in salary disparities. The attractiveness of this approach continues because it is easy to administer, teachers can predict their salaries, and teachers claim that it is objective. In addition, attempts to differentiate salary structures have relied on erratic funding and subjective evaluations of untrained administrators, as well as interventions from teacher organizations. As a result, former merit and other incentive pay plans have fared poorly in public education. It is difficult to create acceptable and reliable measurements of merit upon which to reward teachers, when teachers themselves are uncomfortable with this type of recognition.

Today, we must move beyond this level of discomfort to address compensation. Many of the members of the generation of teachers who are retiring were willing to work longer hours at school and even take on second jobs to support their families. Today's decisions to look seriously at pay-for-performance compensation models are market driven, and to ignore these options for teachers is to put school systems in peril of losing good teachers. As we discussed in Chapter 4, teachers in the future generations are not willing to make this sacrifice. They may have experienced through their own parents the stress that is placed on the family in order to have energy necessary for leadership in any organization. New teachers want good working conditions, balance between their personal and professional lives, and reasonable salaries to support their families. Cochran-Smith (2006) states,

> In order to stay in teaching, today's (and tomorrow's) teachers need: school conditions where they are successful and supported, opportunities to work with other educators in professional learning communities rather than in isolation, differentiated leadership and advancement prospects over the course of the career, and good pay for what they do. (p. 20)

Numerous initiatives are driving conversations and actions to seriously consider how teachers can be compensated at different levels. Thousands of teachers have achieved NBPTS certification, and as the numbers increase these teachers will expect to take on leadership with differentiated salary options. In 2005, 20 governors in their state-of-the-state addresses listed teacher compensation as a key educational issue. The U.S. Department of Education allocated $100 million to a Teacher Incentive Fund and allowed funds from Title II of the No Child Left Behind Act to be used for states and school districts to explore alternative salary models (Baratz-Snowden, 2007, p. 4). National centers, such as the National Center on Performance Incentives (www.performance incentives. org), are researching and exploring teacher compensation models. The editors of *Quality Counts,* an annual report of *Education Week,* have added an emphasis on the teaching profession to the factors they consider as they grade states on education. In the 2008 edition *of Quality Counts,* their analysis of salaries found that "teachers earn 88 cents for every dollar earned in 16 comparable occupations, . . . [and] workers in other occupations have a greater chance to earn above-average salaries than do teachers" (*Education Week*, 2008, p. 8). Years of failure to disseminate school reform initiatives have put the focus where most educators know it makes a difference—on the quality of the individual teacher (Slotnik, 2005). Finally, there is emerging evidence from new pay-for-performance plans that they have "the potential to improve teacher quality, address teacher shortages in specific subject areas and schools, and ensure a more equitable distribution of effective teachers" (Chait, 2007, p. 1).

It appears that pay-for-performance models may be here to stay, in contrast to previous attempts at merit pay and stipend pay models. Rather than dismissing compensation models, school system leaders are using the skepticism of past attempts to inform the new models. The focus on the human resources of school systems is essential for moving beyond skepticism to a viable compensation model.

Most organizations view their employees as vital assets to their success. To achieve this success, there are comprehensive human resource plans that align selection, professional learning, and performance appraisal. Educational systems certainly cannot ignore these human resource components, but it is rare that a school system aligns the components to result in a comprehensive support system for personnel. The crisis of recruitment and retention has forced school system leaders to examine their human resource plans and view pay-for-performance as only one component in a systemic reform essential for retaining quality teachers (Heneman & Milanowski, 2004).

Guidelines (see Table 8.4) for effective compensation programs are emerging based on the few state and school system pay-for-performance programs that are available. The programs are designed so that all teachers may participate. These guidelines are essential if we are not going to repeat the failures of past compensation programs, but they take courage to put into place. One guideline found in most programs addresses teacher leadership responsibilities: When teachers take on additional responsibilities to improve student learning in their schools and communities, they are eligible for additional compensation. To expect teachers to assume these additional responsibilities without compensation ignores what we know about the teachers in today's schools.

Pay-for-performance compensation models for teachers break away from the single-salary model to offer teachers opportunities to earn up to $130,000 or more depending on their knowledge and skills, student learning, leadership, and contribution to high-need schools

Table 8.4   Guidelines for Pay-for-Performance Programs

- Compensation is based on improved student performance, which should be measured by multiple strategies rather than a single test score.
- Teachers expand their professional repertoire of what they know and are able to do in order to improve student learning.
- Quality professional development is provided to help teachers gain the knowledge and skills necessary.
- All teachers are eligible for compensation if they meet the expectations of the program.
- Teachers and administrators are significantly involved in the development of the compensation program.
- Evaluators of teachers must be provided quality professional development. In addition, multiple evaluators can ensure validity through interrater agreement.
- Clear communication and professional development help both teachers and administrators effectively participate in the program.
- Compensation may be tied to special needs in local communities.
- When teachers take on additional responsibilities to improve student learning in their schools and communities, they are eligible for additional compensation.

Sources: Baratz-Snowden, 2007; Center for Teaching Quality, 2007; Chait, 2007; Heneman, Milanowski, Kimball, and Odden, 2006; National Institute for Excellence in Teaching, 2007; Slotnik, 2005.

or subject areas (see Table 8.1). In order to earn these substantially higher salaries, teachers must take on leadership roles. Unless the salary schedule includes substantial increases for teachers, there will be reluctance for teachers to buy into the program. In addition, school systems and states must ensure that funding remains available in order to provide these financial incentives so that improving the financial rewards for teachers encourages them to remain near the classroom where their interest and talents rest.

Providing career options and improving compensation plans are important, but unless we also address the working conditions for all teachers there will be few changes. Unless teacher leaders work in healthy school environments where their work is honored, they will continue to retreat from these new roles.

Improving Working Conditions

The possibility of a teacher shortage based on the current and pending retirements of the baby boomer generation forced policymakers to look closely at recruitment and, more importantly, teacher retention.

The consensus is that there is not a teacher shortage, but a teacher retention problem (Ingersoll & Smith, 2003). Predictably, teachers' reasons for not remaining in the profession include salaries, but unfortunately over 50% of those teachers who leave the profession also share they do so to find a job outside education or report dissatisfaction with teaching as a profession. In a recent *Quality Counts* report, Viadero (2008) stated that "working conditions trump pay" (p. 32). As we discussed in Chapter 5, adult relationships, organizational structure, and principal leadership are significant if teacher leadership is to thrive.

Currently, seven states and one school district in Nevada partner with the Center for Teaching Quality to examine school working conditions in order to better understand how teachers view their workplaces. The Teacher Working Conditions Survey is administered online biannually to both teachers and school administrators, and the public has access to the survey results, so the instrument is a tool for leadership accountability. Teacher leaders were instrumental in the original design of the Teacher Working Conditions Survey. A professional standards commission composed solely of teacher leaders developed and influenced policymakers to administer the first survey and publicly publish the results in North Carolina. The areas that are measured on the survey go beyond class size and teacher/student ratios to focus on working conditions important to all teachers, but especially teacher leaders. Assessed domains include leadership, professional development, empowerment, facilities/resources, and time (Center for Teaching Quality, 2008).

An example of how the results of the Teacher Working Conditions Survey influenced policy was a decision by the North Carolina's State Board of Education to revise the license renewal requirements for school administrators. The new principal license renewal requirements include a "focus on teacher effectiveness, teacher support, teacher leadership, teacher empowerment, and teacher retention" (North Carolina State Board of Education, 2005). Although school, school system, and state responses to improving working conditions are somewhat limited, at least now there is public recognition that if quality teachers are a goal for every student, then policymakers must attend to the conditions of the workplace. As professionals, teachers should no longer work under conditions that provide minimal resources, restrict opportunities for adult collaboration, and give insufficient time for professional needs.

We examined only three areas that teacher leaders claim are concerns in their careers, but there are certainly other areas, such as measures for accountability or time available for teacher leaders. Regardless of the issues, teachers can advocate for their beliefs; in fact, they are often the most influential when working with policymakers at the school district, state, and national levels. In order to do this, though, teachers must learn advocacy skills. One component of leadership is advocacy, and there are skills teachers can learn to influence at the policy level.

Teacher Leaders as Advocates for Change

It is much easier to expect "others" to make changes, but depending on someone else to solve problems is futile. The strongest potential for advocacy is within teachers themselves, and the solutions rely on the deliberate actions of teacher leaders who are realistic about the current problems and potential obstacles yet still find ways to work with their colleagues and others in productive ways.

Teachers tell us that they are still building their self-confidence to be leaders. Speaking up in meetings, taking the initiative to approach the principal with a plan, or buffering their school-site efforts from mandates by district staff are all accomplishments that require teachers to stretch. Teacher leaders who take those risks report the positive feelings they experience when they invite another, less experienced teacher into their classrooms to observe, when they can defend a position in a school improvement team meeting, or when they facilitate a difficult group to work together and reach consensus.

Today, there are avenues in which teacher leaders are learning to be advocates. A few teacher education programs, such at Center X at the University of California, are preparing students to be teacher leaders who advocate for social justice, especially in urban communities. The Center for Teacher Leadership, located at the Virginia Commonwealth University, supports teacher leaders who want to advocate for change. NBPTS-certified teachers, who recognize their own accomplishments, are organized into groups to influence policies at the local, state, and national levels. In 2006, five states held separate summits that engaged NBPTS-certified teachers in discussion focused on recruiting and retaining quality teachers in high-need schools. Outcomes from their work included reports with recommendations and online discussions that lasted throughout the year (Center for Teaching Quality, 2007). In other instances, NBPTS-certified teachers take the initiative to form their own support groups that lead to advocacy for teacher and student learning.

There are resources teacher leaders can turn to for their own professional learning. The Association for Supervision and Curriculum

Development (www.ascd.org) put together an *Advocacy Tool Kit* that provides the information teacher leaders can use to influence policy-makers, the media, and the community. The toolkit offers specific instructions on how to speak in front of a group of policy makers, what to write in an editorial and how to get it published, and other strategies that most lay people do not know. Another provider of this type of support is the Center for Science Education (http://cse.edc.org/prod ucts/teacher leadership), which offers a Web site that helps teacher leaders make presentations, work with the community, write for publication, and develop other advocacy skills.

Over 300 teacher leaders are members of the Teacher Leaders Network (TLN). The TLN Web site states that these teacher leaders are "refining their policy insights and contributing their voices to the decisions that affect the students and communities they serve" (TLN, 2009). This is a powerful group of teacher leaders who are already identified for their competence and credibility. Members of this group write for mass media publications like *Teacher Magazine* (www.teachermagazine.org), attend state and national policy meetings, and participate in an daily discussions as part of a virtual professional community. These are but a few examples of the ways teacher leaders are supporting each other to build their advocacy skills.

Policies and practices that negate teachers' being heard and being fully involved in decisions are changing. Contractual agreements that keep teachers from being full partners in the educational change process with administrators and other stakeholders need to be revisited. Being able to waive policies and rules in order to allow schools to do what is best for children is a critical step to ensure positive efforts and commitment from classroom teachers. Involvement of teachers in setting standards, not just trying to reach them, is important if teachers are to move out of roles as technicians and into professional leadership roles. Teachers can advocate with state legislatures to funnel significant resources to fund pay-for-performance compensations plans, ensure better working conditions, and offer opportunities for quality professional learning. Teachers' voices and views must be heard in the school and at the policy level of districts and states if we are to retain high-quality teachers and improve student learning.

Conclusion

Several factors are critical in forwarding the cause of teacher leadership. First, the educational leaders in the schools and school districts must be committed to instituting teacher leadership by understanding the concept, increasing the awareness of teachers themselves of their leadership potential, and then providing for the development of teacher leadership. In addition, career opportunities for all teachers must become part of the organizational structure so that taking on additional leadership responsibilities is rewarded and recognized as legitimate. Simultaneously, a comprehensive compensation plan should parallel multiple career paths. Finally, the school contexts must reflect working conditions in which teachers can develop and be sustained in leadership roles.

As teacher leadership evolves, continuous efforts are needed to resolve issues and remove barriers to take full advantage of this resource. At times, it seems that teacher leadership has survived in spite of circumstances that blocked its potential and hindered its effectiveness. The benefits of teacher leadership are numerous and significantly enhance the school reform efforts. Recognizing that reform requires persistent work compels us to capitalize on the skills, knowledge, and expertise of every teacher who can be an agent of change. Ultimately, the schools of the future will look quite different from the schools of today. The evolution of teacher leadership will help to make this a positive difference.

Many changes are needed. The status of teachers will be improved when teacher leadership is the norm and when we never again hear the phrase *just a teacher* uttered by a state commissioner of education, a local school board member, a superintendent, or especially by teachers themselves.

Resource A

A Resource for Teacher Leadership: Philosophy of Education Inventory© (PEI©)

Lorraine M. Zinn

Lifelong Learning Options, Quincy, Illinois

As a profession, teaching has become a rather complex endeavor. Schools—and teachers—are expected to address a multitude of social issues and personal needs of students, while continuing to provide the "basics" of a "good education." How can we best educate our children? How are we to make difficult choices about education?

School districts and entire communities argue about what schools are supposed to do and how they should do it. School boards are split into factions, with ardent supporters of "outcome-based education" pitted against "back-to-basics" proponents. After much debate, junior high schools become middle schools; then the middle school concept is reexamined. Many parents and community leaders believe that schools should be teaching students about sex, violence, drug abuse, and other crucial social issues; others believe just as strongly that these issues should be addressed by parents, churches, youth clubs, and various community agencies.

Underlying the heated discussions about these issues is the crucial question: "What is the purpose of education?" Educational philosophy offers a basis for clarifying the purpose(s) of education. Teachers and schools do not engage in the business of education without some underlying purpose, even if the purpose is not explicitly articulated (Zinn, 1991).

Relevance of Educational Philosophy

Educational philosophy offers a means by which educational purpose(s) can be articulated. A *philosophy of education* represents a comprehensive and interrelated set of values and beliefs as applied to education—beliefs about the purpose and nature of human life, the role of the individual in society, purposes or goals of learning and education, role(s) of teachers and students, important subject matter, and effective teaching approaches.

Differences in educational philosophy lead to different forms of education. For example, early American public education focused both on teaching basic literacy ("the 3 R's") and reinforcing prevailing (Christian) beliefs about what was "good" and "right." The Black Studies programs of the late 1960s were designed to instill and reinforce ethnic pride; more recently, multicultural studies have highlighted and positively reinforced the cultural diversity within our society. Maria Montessori's teaching system was developed to encourage individual growth rather than to socialize or "indoctrinate" children. "Back-to-basics" schools reflect a belief that the foundation of a good education includes a solid grounding in reading, writing, and mathematics. Environmental education is, to a great extent, a "consciousness-raising" effort designed to influence major changes at all levels of our society.

The most familiar educational philosophy may be the Progressive approach generally attributed to Dewey (1916/1966), who proposed a dramatic departure from the traditional, or Conservative, approach to education. Other educational philosophies have evolved over the years, with different names and classification schemes. Regardless of their differences, all educational philosophies reflect values and beliefs about certain aspects of education (Apps, 1973; O'Neill, 1981/1990; Zinn, 1983):

- **Purpose(s)** (or goals) of education
- **Content (subject matter)** to be taught or emphasized
- **Methods** of instruction and evaluation

- **Teacher** role(s)
- **Student or learner** role(s) and characteristics

The reason there are multiple educational philosophies is that educators (and parents, legislators, school board members, educational theorists, etc.) hold a wide range of beliefs and values about each of these aspects of education.

A Personal Philosophy of Education

Major decisions about the purpose(s) and direction of education are typically made at the school district level, or even at state and national levels. More recently, some of the decision-making responsibility has been delegated to individual schools, with input from teachers, parents, and other community representatives. Yet there is still an element of choice for individual teachers when it comes to such things as what to emphasize when teaching, what to downplay or avoid, what materials to use, how to assess learning, and so forth.

A teacher may ask him or herself questions such as:

- Given the designated school curriculum, are there sections I think I should emphasize more than others?
- Which classroom materials will I use? If given limited or no choice, how will I use the assigned materials? What else might I add to them?
- Will I use teaching strategies that focus more on individual or collaborative learning?
- How much do I want to challenge my students as learners, and how much do I want to nurture their individual growth and development?
- What are the most important things I can teach my students? If I have to let something else go, what will it be?

Answers to such questions can be found, at least in part, in a teacher's personal philosophy of education.

Why a Personal Educational Philosophy for Teacher Leaders?

There are several compelling reasons why teachers should be encouraged to develop their own personal philosophies of education.

- Educational philosophy offers a foundation on which to base important decisions about curriculum, instruction, and evaluation. In daily lesson planning and classroom teaching, it is the teacher who makes such decisions.
- There is a wealth of information for teachers about what to teach and how to teach, but relatively little information on why teachers should cover particular content and use particular methods. A personal educational philosophy provides a "touchstone" for teachers to remind themselves why they do what they do.
- Exploring educational philosophy can reveal areas of inconsistency or disagreement among teachers or between an individual teacher and the school or district and can also reveal areas of common ground and mutually supportive beliefs. All of these insights are valuable to teachers.
- Teachers are likely to be better leaders in their schools and districts if they understand how educational philosophy affects education and if they are able to share this understanding with other teachers, parents, school administrators, and school boards.

Specifically, a personal philosophy of education offers several benefits:

- An integrated, consistent basis for making educational judgments and decisions
- A framework for asking better questions and for answering questions better, in terms of education
- Assistance in distinguishing between what is worthwhile and what is trivial and what is more or less important
- Expanded vision and enhanced meaning in one's life and work
- Greater congruence between a teacher's beliefs or values and the actions taken and decisions made on a day-to-day basis
- Insight into relationships between teacher and learner, and among learners, subject matter and the world outside of school
- A basis for mutual understanding and productive working relationships among members of an instructional "team," and between teachers and school administrators (Zinn, 1991, pp. 44–45)

Philosophy of Education Inventory©

How can a teacher develop a personal philosophy of education? Is it time to sit down with pen and paper (or computer) and create a series of "I believe . . ." statements about students, subject matter, teaching strategies, and educational purposes? Actually, there is an easier way to clarify one's personal educational philosophy, using a self-assessment tool that links beliefs and values to educational decisions and practices. A copy of the *Philosophy of Education Inventory* (PEI[©]; Zinn, 1999) has been reprinted at the end of this Resource.

Before going any further in your reading, you may want to take a few minutes to complete and score the PEI[©]. Then come back and find out more about your personal philosophy of education.

Interpreting Your Results

What did you discover? Were you surprised? Or did the results confirm what you have generally believed to be your philosophical orientation? Do you recognize the various teaching methods, buzz words, educational practices, and theorists associated with your primary philosophical orientation? A bit more information and a few examples might be helpful in interpreting your results on the PEI[©].

Are the Labels and Scores Important?

Five prevailing philosophies of education have been identified in the PEI[©], using commonly understood titles or labels: Behavioral, Comprehensive, Progressive, Humanistic, and Social Change philosophies of education.[1] These labels distinguish one philosophy from another and validate teachers' beliefs and values as being representative of generally recognized and respected educational philosophies.

However, the intention of the PEI[©] is not to *label* or be *labeled*. This is not a test or a contest in which higher scores are somehow better. The primary focus should be on exploring one's beliefs and values in the context of daily decisions and choices faced by all educators. If the labels and scores further teachers' understanding of educational philosophy and its relevance to teaching, then they are useful; if they get in the way and make people feel as if they're trapped in a box, then the labels and scores are not useful and should be considered relatively unimportant.

Behavioral Philosophy

From a Behavioral standpoint, the primary purpose of education is to teach children to comply with certain standards or expectations set by societal leaders or professional experts. Behaviorism in education emphasizes control, behavioral modification, learning through reinforcement, and management by objectives (Anthony, 1993, p. 1). The focus of instruction might be to teach *right* from *wrong* (e.g., religious catechism), to teach a procedure or sequence of steps (e.g., the correct way to operate a piece of equipment), or even to teach people to obey instructions without questioning authority (e.g., military training). Behavioral educational philosophy tends to support societal values such as productivity, technology, efficiency, and measurability, whereas it is not particularly supportive of progress, change, individualism, and self-reliance (Podeschi, 1986, p. 5).

Generally, Behavioral education relies on step-by-step teaching methods in which one skill must be mastered before another is started, and it incorporates a lot of practice with feedback and (positive or negative) reinforcement. The Behavioral philosophy of education is more closely aligned with vocational education than with an American Literature or Music Appreciation course, and it is more compatible with teaching young children basic mathematics than teaching high school students to use math concepts to make financial projections.

Comprehensive Philosophy

The Comprehensive philosophy of education is symbolized by a liberal arts approach, the primary purpose of which is to provide a broad-based general education rather than a specialized or vocational education. The emphasis in this philosophy is on liberal learning, organized knowledge, and the development of the intellectual powers of the mind (Anthony, 1993, p. 1). Comprehensive education focuses on "shared cultural values, including notions of a common history, common political and economic attitudes, common languages, and a common vision of the future" (Howard, 1992, p. 2). Societal values such as progress, change, newness, optimism, activity, practicality, efficiency, measurability, and technology are not strongly represented in the Comprehensive philosophy of education (Podeschi, 1986, p. 5).

In recent years, this approach to education has often been dismissed as being outdated and irrelevant, partly because of its reliance on noninteractive teaching methods (e.g., lecture and note taking) and its emphasis on historical content rather than current societal issues. However, there is more to this philosophy than the rote transmission of cultural content. Inherent in a Comprehensive educational philosophy is the importance of integrating knowledge acquisition with development of intellectual abilities (e.g., critical and creative thinking skills) and a conceptual understanding of ideas and values (e.g., how history, literature, psychology, sociology, and politics are all relevant to understanding book censorship). A recent example of the reemergence of the Comprehensive educational philosophy is the Paideia Program, which has as its basic premise the belief that "all genuine learning arises from the activity of the learner's own mind. . . . When the activities performed by the teacher render students passive, the latter cease to be learners, memorizers perhaps, but not learners" (Adler, 1984, p. 47). Some of today's alternative public schools, as well as many long-standing private schools, have been founded on a Comprehensive philosophy of education.

Progressive Philosophy

The primary focus of Progressive educational philosophy is educating people to live responsibly and resolve problems cooperatively within a democratic society. The term Progressive may seem to be a misnomer, yet in the early years of this century (Dewey, 1916/1966), it was immediately recognizable as the antithesis of *conservative* or *traditional* (liberal arts) education. Essential elements of Progressive philosophy include a commitment to teaching children to be responsible citizens, emphasizing real-life experience in the learning process, making schools and classrooms into communities of learning, encouraging active inquiry on the part of children, and developing schools that can embrace cultural difference instead of smothering it (Featherstone, 1991, p. x).

Currently, Progressive educational philosophy is evidenced through cooperative learning efforts, community service projects, multicultural education, authentic assessment, and the school improvement teams of teachers and parents who have assumed some of the planning and decision-making responsibilities formerly reserved for school boards and administrators. A primary role of the teacher in a Progressive education is *guidance:* "assisting through cooperation the natural capacities of the individuals guided" (Dewey, 1916/1966, p. 23). An example of this *guidance/cooperation* concept put into practice is Group Investigation,

> a cooperative learning strategy that integrates interaction and communication in the classroom with the process of academic inquiry. It enables the classroom to become a social system built both on cooperation among students in small groups and on coordination between groups in the classroom. (Sharan & Sharan, 1992, p. ix)

In recent years, the concept of *education for democracy* seems to be interpreted primarily as cooperative learning and realistic learning experiences designed to prepare children to live in the world outside of school. However, educational programs focusing on drug awareness, domestic and societal violence, and sex education do encourage children to be responsible citizens in a democratic society.

Humanistic Philosophy

Humanistic education is sometimes referred to as education for self-actualization, or "self-initiated development of a person's skills and potentials to lead to a fulfilling life of challenge and growth" (Gross, 1991, p. 33). Humanistic philosophy is strongly aligned with Abraham Maslow's psychology of human motivation, in which self-actualization is considered to be the ultimate goal of human development. *Humanism* emphasizes freedom and autonomy, trust, cooperation, participation, and self-directed learning (Anthony, 1993, p. 1). Humanistic educational philosophy tends to support societal values such as individualism and self-reliance, whereas it is not particularly supportive of productivity, technology, efficiency, and measurability (Podeschi, 1986, p. 5). The primary focus of Humanistic education is to support and facilitate the personal growth and development of each individual student. An example of this philosophy is the recent trend toward inclusion of all students in regular classrooms, rather than putting *less-abled* or *physically or developmentally challenged* students in *special education* classes. (Notice how even the descriptive terms have changed?)

A recent study of the relationship between "teacher belief systems" and teacher effectiveness identified a number of teacher beliefs as being humanistic in nature: "trust, acceptance, friendship, respect, self-discipline, democratic climate, flexibility, student self-determination, and nonpunitive, nonmoralistic attitudes" (Agne, Greenwood, & Miller, 1994, p. 149).

A basic assumption of the Humanistic educational philosophy is that "human nature is essentially good" (Elias & Merriam, 1995, p. 117). A fundamental orientation of Humanistic educational philosophy is the concept of caring, which is strongly supported by Noddings (1992), author of *The Challenge to Care in Schools*. Noddings (1992) suggests that school curricula be completely reorganized "around themes of caring for self, for intimate others, for strangers and global others, for the natural world and its non-human creatures, for the human-made world, and for ideas" (p. 675).

Social Change Philosophy

This philosophy views education as a primary force for transforming society, and it emphasizes freedom and autonomy of the learner. A major theme of Social Change philosophy is a recognition of the influences of cultural, political, and economic factors on individuals and groups. Social change education "generally runs against the current of American value patterns, . . . pushing for political consciousness and social action, [emphasizing] knowledge as power and a partnership between teachers and students" (Podeschi, 1986, p. 5). At its core, Social Change philosophy would go beyond the mainstream belief in equality of opportunity to support equality of societal conditions. Examples of this philosophy of education include the *descholing* movement associated with Illich, the *critical consciousness* pedagogy of Freire, Shor's notion of *empowering education* (Shor, 1992), and resistance to state and federal authority over schools, including the current reemergence of opposition to compulsory education.

Multiple Philosophical Orientations

As assessed on the PEI©, teachers tend either to have a clear primary philosophical orientation (represented by a score of 75 or higher) or to share two philosophies that are stronger (i.e., have higher scores) than others. Typical combinations are Behavioral-Comprehensive and Progressive-Humanistic. Less typical, though still compatible combinations, are Behavioral-Progressive and Progressive-Social Change. Unlikely combinations would be Behavioral-Humanistic and Behavioral-Social Change, given that the basic values underlying these philosophies are essentially incompatible.

Generally, more experienced teachers have a clearly defined philosophy (i.e., scores of at least 75 on one or two as compared to the others). Less experienced teachers often find that their scores are fairly equal among three or more of the philosophies, because their own beliefs and values about education may still be developing and may still be mingled with beliefs and values held by their parents, peers, or college instructors.

Regardless of experience, if there is no clear preference (i.e., no fairly high score) for one or two of the philosophies, or if the highest scores represent essentially incompatible philosophies, teachers could benefit from further exploration and clarification of their personal beliefs and values about education. It would be especially helpful to look for contradictions among statements on the PEI© that had the highest individual ratings (i.e., a rating of 6 or 7 on any single sentence-completion item).

What About Teaching Style?

Is *personal educational philosophy* the same as *teaching style?* These two concepts are certainly interrelated, though probably not identical. Heimlich and Norland (1994) suggest that "teaching style is how you philosophically approach and then conduct . . . instruction" (p. 43). "Style is a mode of expression. . . . [It] has to do with form rather than content, process rather than product" (p. 40). *Teaching style* evolves as a combination of one's educational philosophy and preferred teaching methods, techniques, and strategies.

Educational philosophy is primarily concerned with *why* teachers do what they do, whereas methods, techniques, and strategies describe and guide *what* teachers do. Educational philosophies are fairly deeply rooted in people's life values and are unlikely to change significantly. Teaching methods, techniques, and strategies, on the other hand, may change depending on what works best in a particular situation.

Certain methods and techniques are more strongly supportive of a particular philosophy (e.g., cooperative learning as representative of Progressive philosophy, or group discussion as representative of Humanistic philosophy). However, a skilled teacher may selectively mix and match a variety of methods, techniques, and strategies, as long as they are not inconsistent with the basic premise of a given philosophy. Examples of a mismatch would be extensive use of lecture and rote learning within a Progressive or Humanistic philosophy, or group discussion as a primary technique to support Behavioral education.

Next Steps and Practical Applications

Developing a Statement of Educational Philosophy

Sometimes teachers are asked to describe their Philosophy of Education in narrative form (e.g., on a job application or in an interview). The PEI© can be used as a starting point for developing such a statement. Here's an example of a way to approach the task.

1. Decide whether you identify strongly enough with any one of the five philosophies to say something such as, "My Educational Philosophy is basically Humanistic (Progressive,

Behavioral, etc.)." An alternative would be to identify two closely related philosophies as being strong influences, for example, Humanistic-Progressive or Comprehensive-Behavioral.

2. Using the *Philosophy of Education Inventory,* select all of the responses you rated 6 or 7, and start to create your narrative by rewriting those items as complete sentences (e.g., for Item 8 on the PEI©, you might write, "In planning an educational activity, I try to create a supportive climate that facilitates self-discovery and interaction").

3. Organize these sentences in a way that starts to shape a coherent narrative. One way to group them would be according to the five elements mentioned earlier as being inherent in any statement of educational philosophy: Purpose(s) (or goals) of education, Content (subject matter) to be taught or emphasized, Methods of instruction and evaluation, Teacher role(s), and Student or Learner role(s) and characteristics. You may want to create some additional or different groupings.

4. Examine this draft statement carefully, looking for contradictions. For example, it would be inconsistent to hold equally strong beliefs about the need for teacher control and for student autonomy, or for a problem-oriented curriculum and a lock-step curriculum. If you find such contradictions, continue to reflect on what you believe and rewrite, delete, or add specific sentences until the statements within your educational philosophy are more internally consistent.

5. Finally, revise your Educational Philosophy statement so that it is well organized and grammatically correct. As much as possible, use language that describes your decisions and actions as a teacher, rather than statements about your beliefs. (Remember that your beliefs and values are reflected in your decisions and actions.)

CAUTION: Many teachers want to create an eclectic educational philosophy, selecting particular ideas, theories, and techniques from a wide range of choices and putting them together to form a unique entity. Current trends in American education support this approach, based on the prevailing attitude that schools can, and should, "do it all." This is an admirable intention, yet it may not be feasible. Some beliefs about education are incompatible with each other, and others are even diametrically opposed. For example, from a Behavioral viewpoint, "Students learn best when the educational activity provides for practice and repetition." This concept is radically different from a Humanistic viewpoint, which suggests that "Students learn best when they are free to explore, without the constraints of a *system*." With an eclectic approach, then, it is important that the individual "bits and pieces" of the resulting educational philosophy be consistent with its basic premises.

Strengthening the Instructional Team

The *Philosophy of Education Inventory* is a valuable staff development tool for instructional teams (teachers, curriculum planners, administrators, etc.). It offers a way to defuse tension and clear up misunderstandings among people who may not see eye to eye with each other. After completing the PEI© and sharing information about the results, instructional teams have reported that they could let go of the feeling of "I'm right and you're wrong" and accept that each person has somewhat different beliefs and values about education. Recognizing and validating both differences and commonalities usually leads to better understanding and communication, improved working relationships among coworkers, and more effective educational planning and decision making, all of which ultimately benefit students.

Walking the Talk

Even when people have the best of intentions, it is not unusual to find discrepancies between what people say they *believe* and what they actually do. Argyris and Schön (1974) tried to figure out why people have difficulty changing their actions, even when they apparently want to change. This difficulty may represent a conflict between something called *theories-in-use* (long-held beliefs and values that strongly influence actions) and *espoused theories* (the things people say they believe and value). Espoused theories and theories-in-use are often incompatible, yet people don't recognize it! Apparently, human nature supports a fairly strong desire to keep old theories-in-use.

Becoming aware of discrepancies between what we say we *believe* and what we actually *do* as teachers could offer some valuable insights. The PEI© offers a way to start this self-assessment. After completing the Inventory, you might want to review your answers with a colleague and invite her or him to observe your teaching and give you some feedback on specific areas in which your actions seem to be fairly congruent—or incongruent—with your stated beliefs.

Teachers as Leaders

Teacher leaders can use information and insights from the PEI© as a foundation for decisions in developing curriculum, selecting instructional strategies, and establishing assessment methods. An exploration of educational philosophy can help members of a school community understand why they make certain choices and why they sometimes disagree about how best to educate children. Clarification of personal educational philosophies may reveal areas of incongruence between individual teacher beliefs and values and the operating assumptions of their schools. Teacher leaders can help colleagues explore differences and build a stronger shared vision.

Teachers can be even stronger leaders if they are clear about their values and beliefs and strive to act in congruence with those values and beliefs. Ultimately, it is *teachers* who will have some of the best answers to that tough question posed earlier: "How can we best educate our children?" Having a clear sense of one's personal philosophy of education can lead to some pretty good answers!

Philosophy of Education Inventory©

Instructions

Each of the 15 items on the Inventory begins with an incomplete sentence, followed by five different options that might complete the sentence. Underneath each option is a scale from 1 to 7, followed by a small letter in parentheses. For the present, ignore the small letters; use only the small numbers on the scale.

To complete the Inventory, read each sentence stem and each optional phrase that completes it. On the 1-to-7 scale, circle the number that most closely indicates how you feel about each option. The scale goes from 1 (*strongly disagree*) to 7 (*strongly agree*), with a *neutral* point (4) if you don't have any opinion or are not sure about a particular option.

Continue through all the items, reading the sentence stem and indicating how strongly you agree or disagree with each of the options. Please respond to every option, even if you feel neutral about it. THERE ARE NO RIGHT OR WRONG ANSWERS.

As you go through the Inventory, respond according to what you most frequently or most likely do. If it helps you to respond more easily, you may want to focus on a specific course that you teach. If you do focus on a particular course, choose one that you feel most comfortable teaching—one that you think best reflects your preferred way(s) of teaching.
HAVE FUN!

STRONGLY DISAGREE		NEUTRAL		STRONGLY AGREE		
1	2	3	4	5	6	7

1. IN PLANNING AN EDUCATIONAL ACTIVITY, I AM MOST LIKELY TO:

Clearly identify the results I want and develop a class or program that will achieve those results.

1	2	3	4	5	6	7(c)

Identify—with equal participation from students—significant social, cultural, political or economic issues and plan learning activities that will help the students contribute to social change.

1	2	3	4	(5)	6	7(h)

Begin by choosing content or subject matter that is likely to benefit students for the rest of their lives.

1	2	3	4	5	6	(7(a))

Make sure educational activities are practical and relevant to students' lives outside of school.

1	2	3	4	5	6	(7(d))

Find out what is of greatest interest to students and plan educational activities around those interests, even if I may not agree with them.

1	2	(3)	4	5	6	7(f)

STRONGLY DISAGREE		NEUTRAL		STRONGLY AGREE		
1	2	3	4	5	6	7

2. STUDENTS LEARN BEST:

When new knowledge is presented from a problem-solving approach.

1	2	3	4	5	6	(7(x))

When the educational activity is clearly structured and provides for practice and repetition.

1	2	3	4	(5)	6	7(w)

Through open discussion and critical reflection with others, both inside and outside of school.

1   2   3   4   5   6   (7(z))

When they can make self-directed choices about learning methods and outcomes.

1   2   3   4   5   6   (7(y))

From an "expert" who knows what he or she is talking about.

1   2   3   (4)   5   6   7(v)

STRONGLY DISAGREE		NEUTRAL		STRONGLY AGREE		
1	2	3	4	5	6	7

3. THE PRIMARY PURPOSE OF EDUCATION IS:

To facilitate the personal growth and development of each student.

1   2   3   4   5   6   (7(f))

To increase students' awareness of the need for significant change in our culture and society, and to help them contribute to such change.

1   2   3   4   5   (6)   7(h)

To teach a broad range of content, concepts, and principles that will prepare students for learning throughout life.

1   2   3   4   (5)   6   7(a)

To increase students' problem-solving skills and ability to fully participate in the society in which they live.

1   2   3   4   5   6   (7(d))

To develop students' competency and mastery of specific knowledge and skills, so they can meet certain standards or expectations.

1   2   3   4   (5)   6   7(c)

STRONGLY DISAGREE		NEUTRAL		STRONGLY AGREE		
1	2	3	4	5	6	7

4. THE MOST VALUABLE THINGS PEOPLE KNOW:

Are learned by studying or working cooperatively with others, solving problems along the way.

1   2   3   4   5   **(6)**   7(x)

Are learned through reflective thinking focused on important issues and questions about our culture and society—past, present, and future.

1   2   ·3   4   **(5)**   6   7(z)

Are learned through a structured educational approach that consistently helps them to find the right answers.

1   2   **(3)**   4   5   6   7(w)

Are gained through self-discovery rather than some "teaching" process.

1   2   3   4   5   **(6)**   7(y)

Are learned through a broad-based educational process rather than specialized or career-oriented education.

1   2   3   **(4)**   5   6   7(v)

STRONGLY DISAGREE		NEUTRAL		STRONGLY AGREE		
1	2	3	4	5	6	7

5. I CHOOSE THE CONTENT I WILL TEACH BASED ON:

Consultation with students about what is most important or interesting to them.

1   2   3   4   **(5)**   6   7(f)

What I believe students need to learn next, in comparison with what they already know.

1   2   3   4   5   6   **(7(c))**

Current social, cultural, political, or economic situations and issues.

1   2   3   4   **(5)**   6   7(h)

A consideration of students' "real-life" needs and problems outside the classroom.

1   2   3   4   5   6   **7(d)**

Generally agreed-upon subject matter for a "well-rounded" education.

1   2   3   4   5   **6**   7(a)

STRONGLY DISAGREE		NEUTRAL		STRONGLY AGREE		
1	2	3	4	5	6	7

6. THE BEST TEACHERS START PLANNING INSTRUCTION:

By considering the specific outcomes (knowledge, skills, and attitudes) they are looking for and the most effective ways of achieving these outcomes.

1   2   3   4   5   6   **7(w)**

By identifying everyday problems that can be solved as a result of the instruction.

1   2   3   4   5   **6**   7(x)

By clarifying the content, concepts, and theoretical principles to be taught.

1   2   3   4   5   **6**   7(v)

By identifying cultural, social, political, or economic issues that have the greatest impact on the lives of students and their families.

1   2   3   4   **5**   6   7(z)

By asking students to identify what they want to learn and how they want to learn it.

1   2   3   **4**   5   6   7(y)

STRONGLY DISAGREE		NEUTRAL		STRONGLY AGREE		
1	2	3	4	5	6	7

7. AS AN EDUCATOR, I AM MOST SUCCESSFUL IN SITUATIONS:

That are unstructured and flexible enough to follow students' interests.

1   2   **3**   4   5   6   7(f)

That are well structured, with clear behavioral objectives and built-in feedback loops for students.

1   2   3   4   5   6   (7(c))

Where I can focus on practical skills and knowledge that students can put to use in real life.

1   2   3   4   5   (6)   7(d)

Where I can organize the subject matter in a logical way and build a solid foundation for future learning.

1   2   3   4   5   6   (7(a))

Where the students are willing to explore and critically reflect on what is going on in the world around them.

1   2   3   4   5   (6)   7(h)

STRONGLY DISAGREE		NEUTRAL		STRONGLY AGREE		
1	2	3	4	5	6	7

8. IN PLANNING AN EDUCATIONAL ACTIVITY, I TRY TO CREATE:

An opportunity for students to make application of new knowledge, concepts, and skills to "real-world" situations.

1   2   3   4   5   (6)   7(x)

A setting in which students are encouraged to examine their beliefs and values and to raise critical questions.

1   2   3   4   5   (6)   7(z)

A structured environment that keeps students focused and moves them systematically toward the intended learning outcomes.

1   2   3   4   5   6   (7(w))

A conceptual understanding of the breadth and depth of what is to be learned.

1   2   3   4   5   (6)   7(v)

A supportive climate that facilitates self-discovery and interaction.

1   2   3   4   5   6   (7(y))

STRONGLY DISAGREE		NEUTRAL		STRONGLY AGREE		
1	2	3	4	5	6	7

9. STUDENTS' FEELINGS DURING THE LEARNING PROCESS:

Are crucial to the learning process and must be brought to the surface in order for students to fully engage in any learning activity.

1   2   3   4   5   6   **7(h)**

Provide energy that can be focused on problems or questions.

1   2   3   4   5   **6**   7(d)

Reflect the uniqueness of each student and should be expressed and valued in the learning process.

1   2   3   4   5   6   **7(f)**

Are likely to get in the way of learning by diverting the students' attention.

1   2   3   **4**   5   6   7(c)

Are not as important as what students are thinking.

1   **2**   3   4   5   6   7(a)

STRONGLY DISAGREE		NEUTRAL		STRONGLY AGREE		
1	2	3	4	5	6	7

10. THE TEACHING METHODS I PREFER:

Focus on problem solving and present real challenges to the students.

1   2   3   4   **5**   6   7(x)

Emphasize practice and offer constructive feedback so that students can get the right answers and learn essential skills.

1   **2**   3   4   5   6   7(w)

Are mostly nondirective, encouraging students to take responsibility for their own learning.

1   2   3   **4**   5   6   7(y)

Involve students in discussion and critical examination of controversial issues.

| 1 | 2 | 3 | 4 | 5 | 6 | (7)(z) |

Are designed to help students develop effective thinking and reasoning abilities.

| 1 | 2 | 3 | 4 | 5 | 6 | (7)(v) |

STRONGLY DISAGREE		NEUTRAL		STRONGLY AGREE		
1	2	3	4	5	6	7

11. WHEN STUDENTS ARE UNINTERESTED IN A SUBJECT, IT IS BECAUSE:

They don't realize how seriously the issue(s) being studied may affect their lives and their future.

| 1 | 2 | 3 | 4 | 5 | (6) | 7(h) |

They don't see any benefit for their daily lives outside of school.

| 1 | 2 | 3 | 4 | 5 | (6) | 7(d) |

They are just not "motivated" to learn.

| 1 | 2 | 3 | 4 | (5) | 6 | 7(a) |

They are not "ready" to learn it, or they aren't getting enough practice or feedback.

| 1 | 2 | 3 | 4 | 5 | 6 | (7(c)) |

That subject isn't a high priority for them personally; they are more interested in something else.

| 1 | 2 | 3 | 4 | (5) | 6 | 7(f) |

STRONGLY DISAGREE		NEUTRAL		STRONGLY AGREE		
1	2	3	4	5	6	7

12. DIFFERENCES AMONG STUDENTS:

Are relatively unimportant as long as the students gain a common base of understanding through the educational experience.

| 1 | (2) | 3 | 4 | 5 | 6 | 7(v) |

Enable them to learn best on their own time and in their own way and should be valued and strongly supported.

1   2   3   **(4)**   5   6   7(y)

Are primarily due to differences in their life experiences and will usually lead them to make different applications of new knowledge and skills to their own situations.

1   2   3   4   **(5)**   6   7(x)

Arise from their particular cultural and social situations and are extremely relevant to the educational process.

1   2   3   4   5   6   **(7)(z)**

Will not interfere with their learning if each student is given adequate opportunity for practice and reinforcement.

1   2   3   4   5   **(6)**   7(w)

STRONGLY DISAGREE		NEUTRAL	STRONGLY AGREE		
1	2	3	4	5	6	7

13. EVALUATION OF LEARNING OUTCOMES:

Is not of great importance and is not easily accomplished, because the impact of education should be more evident outside of school than in a classroom.

(1)   2   3   4   5   6   7(h)

Should be built into the educational process so that students continually receive feedback and can adjust their performance accordingly.

1   2   3   4   5   6   **(7)(c)**

Is best done by the students themselves, for their own purposes.

1   2   3   4   **(5)**   6   7(f)

Lets a teacher know how much information and conceptual understanding each student has acquired, in comparison to other students.

1   2   3   4   **(5)**   6   7(a)

Is best accomplished when the student encounters a problem, either in the classroom or in the "real world," and then successfully resolves it.

1   2   3   4   **(5)**   6   7(d)

STRONGLY DISAGREE		NEUTRAL		STRONGLY AGREE		
1	2	3	4	5	6	7

14. MY PRIMARY ROLE AS A TEACHER IS TO:

Set clear expectations and lead students step by step through educational activities with well-directed feedback.

1   2   3   4   5   6   **7(w)**

Introduce students to a broad range of information and ways of thinking about the world.

1   2   3   4   5   6   **7(v)**

Help students "learn how to learn" what is useful for their lives.

1   2   3   4   5   6   **7(x)**

Increase students' awareness of social, cultural, economic, or political issues and help them learn how to have an impact on societal conditions that need to be changed.

1   2   3   4   5   6   **7(z)**

Facilitate, but not direct, learning activities that are meaningful to each student.

1   2   3   4   5   6   **7(y)**

STRONGLY DISAGREE		NEUTRAL		STRONGLY AGREE		
1	2	3	4	5	6	7

15. IN THE END, IF STUDENTS HAVE NOT LEARNED WHAT WAS TAUGHT:

They lacked appreciation for the subject matter, or they found intellectual challenge too demanding.

1   2   3   4   **5**   6   7(a)

They need to repeat one or more educational activities until they can master the learning (or at least meet minimum standards).

1   2   3   **4**   5   6   7(c)

It's okay, because they probably learned something else that they considered just as interesting or important.

1   2   3   4   5   6   7(f)

They don't realize how the new knowledge will empower them to significantly affect the world in which they live.

1   2   3   **4**   5   6   7(h)

It is probably because they are unable to make practical application of what was taught to problems in their daily lives.

1   2   3   4   (5)   6   7(d)

Scoring Instructions

After completing the Inventory, go back to your responses and find the small letter in parentheses to the far right of each rating scale. This is a code letter for scoring the Inventory. Transfer each of your numbers from the rating scales to the Scoring Matrix located on the next page. For example, for item 1, if you circled a 5 for option (h), write the number 5 in the box for 1(h). Item 1 has five different responses: c, h, a, d, and f. Record all five of your responses for item 1, then continue in every other square in the Scoring Matrix (like a checkerboard).

[PLEASE COMPLETE THE SCORING MATRIX Figure A.1]

Now, add all the numbers by columns, from top to bottom, so that you have 10 separate subtotals. None of these subtotals should be higher than 56, nor should any be lower than 7. For TOTAL SCORES, combine the subtotals from the columns on the Scoring Matrix, as indicated in the following. Note: Final scores should be no higher than 105 and no lower than 15.

$$B(c + w) = \underline{88} \quad C(a + v) = \underline{80} \quad P(d + x) = \underline{91}$$
$$H(f + y) = \underline{76} \quad S(h + z) = \underline{87}$$

What Your Scores Mean

1 B = BEHAVIORAL EDUCATION

(Education for Competence, Behavioral Change, Compliance With Standards)

4 C = COMPREHENSIVE EDUCATION

(General Education for Life)

2 P = PROGRESSIVE EDUCATION

(Education for Problem Solving in Society)

5 H = HUMANISTIC EDUCATION

(Education for Individual Self-Actualization)

3 S = SOCIAL CHANGE EDUCATION

(Education for Transforming Society)

Figure A.1   Scoring Matrix

ITEM	c	w	a	v	d	x	f	y	h	z
1	6		5		5		3		4	
2		6		5		6		5		6
3	5		6		5		6		5	
4		6		5		6		6		5
5	6		7		3		3		5	
6		7		5		5		3		4
7	7		7		6		2		6	
8		7		6		6		5		5
9	2		2		6		7		7	
10		7		5		5		3		3
11	4		5		6		5		6	
12		7		2		7		7		7
13	7		5		5		5		4	
14		7		7		7		7		7
15	7		2		3		1		4	
SUB-TOTALS	44	47	39	35	39	42	32	36	41	37
ADD	c + w		a + v		d + x		f + y		h + z	
YOUR SCORES	B = 91		C = 74		P = 81		H = 68		S = 78	

What Is a Philosophy of Education?

A philosophy of education represents a comprehensive and interrelated set of values and beliefs as applied to education—including beliefs about the purpose and nature of human life, the role of the individual in society, purposes and goals of education, role(s) of teachers and students, important subject matter, and effective teaching approaches.

A personal philosophy of education provides an integrated, consistent basis for making choices in the practice of education and offers insight into relationships between and among (a) teachers and learners, (b) learners and learning content-activities, and (c) learning content-activities and the world at large. Identifying one's personal philosophy of education can enhance the degree of congruence between a teacher's beliefs-values and actions in the practice of teaching and can provide a basis for mutual understanding and acceptance among members of an instructional "team," given the great diversity of teachers, program planners, and administrators who make up the field of education.

Table A.1 is an interpretation matrix that briefly describes five different philosophies of education.

At the top of the interpretation matrix (Table A.1, "Five Philosophies of Education"), write your score for each philosophy above the column that describes it. Your highest score reflects the philosophy that is closest to your own beliefs; your lowest score reflects a philosophy that is least like yours. For example, a score of 95–105 indicates that you strongly agree with that philosophy; a score of 15–25 indicates that you strongly disagree with a given philosophy.

Most educators have a clear primary philosophical orientation, or else they share two that are stronger than others. Typical combinations include: Behavioral and Comprehensive, Progressive and Humanistic, Progressive and Social Change, or Humanistic and Social Change. It is quite unlikely that you would have high scores in both Comprehensive and Social Change, or in both Behavioral and Humanistic philosophies. These philosophies have key underlying assumptions that are inherently contradictory. For example, the primary purpose of Behavioral Education is to ensure compliance with expectations or standards set by others, whereas Humanistic Education is intended to enhance individual self-development—which may or may not meet anyone else's expectations or standards.

If you find that your scores are fairly equal among all of the philosophies or are spread among three or more, you may want to spend some time clarifying your beliefs and values and looking for possible contradictions among them.

Table A.1 Five Philosophies of Education

Total Scores:	B = 88	C = 80	P = 91	H = 76	S = 87
	Behavioral	Comprehensive	Progressive	Humanistic	Social Change
Purpose(s)	To promote skill development and behavioral change; ensure compliance with standards and societal expectations	To develop intellectual powers of the mind; to enhance the broadest sense of learning; to provide a general, "well-rounded" education	To support responsible participation in society; to give students practical knowledge and problem-solving skills	To enhance personal growth and development; to facilitate self-actualization	To bring about, through education, fundamental social, cultural, political, and economic change in society
Student(s)	Students not involved in setting objectives; expected to master one step before another; practice behaviors/skills to get them right	"Renaissance person"; cultured; seeks knowledge; expected to gain conceptual and theoretical understanding	Student needs and experiences are valued; all student cultures respected; student takes an active role in learning process	Student is highly motivated and self-directed; assume responsibility for learning; highly involved in planning learning efforts	Equality with teacher in learning process; autonomous; empowered; totally voluntary participant
Teacher Role	Teacher is the manager, controller, authoritarian, sets expectations; predict and direct outcomes	The "expert;" transmitter of knowledge; clearly direct learning process; challenge students to think	Organizer, guides learning process; provides real-life learning applications; helps students work cooperatively	Facilitator; helper; mutual participant in teaching-learning exchange; support learning process	Coordinator; convener; equal partner with learner; makes suggestions only

Concepts/Key Words	Standards-based; mastery learning; performance-based; ability grouping, behavioral objectives; behavioral modification; accountability; core knowledge	Liberal arts; learning for its own sake; general education; critical thinking; traditional knowledge; academic excellence; college prep; tracking systems	Problem-solving; practical learning; experienced based; needs assessment; transfer of learning; active inquiry; collaboration; responsible citizens; democratic ideals; community service	Freedom; autonomy; individuality; teaching-learning exchange; self-directedness; interpersonal-communication; openness; empowerment; authenticity; emotional intelligence	Consciousness-raising; praxis; noncompulsory learning; autonomy; social action; social justice; empowerment; social transformation
Methods	Computer-aided instructor, lock-step curriculum, skill training, demo & practice, criterion-referenced testing	Lecture; critical reading and analysis; question-and-answer, teacher-directed discussion; individual study; standardized testing	Projects; field trips; simulations; group investigation; cooperative learning; thematic curriculum: portfolio assessment	Experience learning; discover learning, open discussion; individual projects; collaborative learning; independent study; self-assessment	Critical discussion; problem-posing; maximum interaction; analysis of media output; sensitivity training

(Continued)

Table A.1 (Continued)

Total Scores:	$B = \underline{24}$	$C = \underline{30}$	$P = \underline{91}$	$H = \underline{76}$	$S = \underline{51}$
	Behavioral	Comprehensive	Progressive	Humanistic	Social Change
People/ Practices	Watson, Skinner, Thorndike, Steinberg, Tyler, Mager, vocation training, special education, certification exams, religious indoctrination, military training, management-by-objectives, "back-to-basics" programs	Aristotle, Socrates, Plato, Adler, Rousseau, Pier, Hutchins, Great Books Society, Essentialist School, Paideia Program, Efficacy Institute, prep schools, junior high schools, gifted & talented programs	Spencer, Whitehead, Dewey, Sizer, Spady, middle schools, mainstreaming, multicultural education, sex education for social responsibility, anti-drug-abuse programs, community internships, authentic assessment	Rogers, Maslow, Patterson, Simpson, Knowles, Summerhill School, Sudbury Valley School, Montessori schools, Waldorf schools, open classrooms, inclusion curriculum, credit for prior learning	Reich, Counts, Neill, Holt, Freire, Illich, Kozol, Shor, Simon, free school movement, deschooling, social action theater, diversity education, voter education, social justice education

There is no right or wrong philosophy of education. The Inventory is designed to reflect back to you some of your own beliefs, not to make judgments about those beliefs. It is up to you to decide how your beliefs may influence your decisions and actions as an educator and how your personal education philosophy may be well suited—or perhaps not the best match—for the educational setting in which you work or for a team-teaching approach.

Note

1. Descriptions are adapted from Elias and Merriam (1995), O'Neill (1981/1990), and Anthony (1993).

References

Adler, M. J. (1984). *The Paideia program: An educational syllabus.* New York: Macmillan.

Agne, K. J., Greenwood, G. E., & Miller, L. D. (1994). Relationship between teacher belief systems and teacher effectiveness. *Journal of Research and Development in Education, 27,* 141–152.

Anthony, L. V. (1993). *Five philosophies of education for grades K–12.* Unpublished manuscript, South Florida Center for Educational Leaders, Davie, FL.

Apps, J. W. (1973). *Towards a working philosophy of adult education (Occasional Paper No. 36).* Syracuse, NY: Syracuse University Publications in Continuing Education and ERIC Clearinghouse on Adult Education.

Argyris, C., & Schön, D. A. (1974). *Theory in practice: Increasing personal effectiveness.* San Francisco: Jossey-Bass.

Dewey, J. (1966). *Democracy and education.* New York: Macmillan. (Original work published 1916)

Elias, J. L., & Merriam, S. B. (1995). *Philosophical foundations of adult education* (2nd ed.). Melbourne, FL: Krieger.

Featherstone, J. (1991). Foreword. In K. Jervis & C. Montag (Eds.), *Progressive education for the 1990s: Transforming practice* (pp. ix–xiii). New York: Teachers College Press.

Gross, R. (1991). *Peak learning: A master course in learning how to learn.* Los Angeles: Jeremy P. Tarcher.

Heimlich, J. E., & Norland, E. (1994). *Developing teaching style in adult education.* San Francisco: Jossey-Bass.

Howard, C. C. (1992). *Theories of general education: A critical approach.* New York: St. Martin's.

Noddings, N. (1992). *The challenge to care in schools.* New York: Teachers College Press.

O'Neill, W. F. (1990). *Educational ideologies: Contemporary expressions of educational philosophy* (Rev. ed.). Dubuque, IA: Kendall/Hunt. (Original work published 1981)

Podeschi, R. L. (1986). Philosophies, practices and American values. *Lifelong Learning: An Omnibus of Practice and Research, 9*(4), 4–6, 27–28.

Sharan, Y., & Sharan, S. (1992). *Expanding cooperative learning through group investigation.* New York: Teachers College Press.

Shor, I. (1992). *Empowering education: Critical teaching for social change.* Chicago: University of Chicago Press.

Zinn, L. M. (1983). Development of a valid and reliable instrument to identify a personal philosophy of adult education. *Dissertation Abstracts International, 44,* 1667A-1668A. (University Microfilms No. DA 8323851).

Zinn, L. M. (1991). Identifying your philosophical orientation. In M. W. Galbraith (Ed.), *Adult learning methods* (Rev. ed., pp. 39–77). Melbourne, FL: Krieger.

Zinn, L. M. (1998). Identifying your philosophical orientation. In M. W. Gailbraith (Ed.), *Adult Learning Methods* (2nd ed., pp. 37–72). Melbourne, FL: Krieger.

Zinn, L. M. (1999). *Philosophy of education inventory* (Rev. ed.). Boulder, CO: Lifelong Learning Options.

Resource B

Teacher Leadership School Survey (TLSS)

Figure B.1   Teacher Leadership School Survey (TLSS)

Teacher Leadership School Survey

Marilyn and Bill Katzenmeyer

Please respond to the following statements in terms of how frequently each statement is descriptive of your school.

Never	Rarely	Some-times	Often	Always

		Never	Rarely	Some-times	Often	Always
1.	At my school administrators and teachers try hard to help new teachers be successful.	1	2	3	4	5
2.	At my school, teachers are provided with assistance, guidance or coaching if needed.	1	2	3	4	5
3.	Administrators at my school actively support the professional development of faculty and staff.	1	2	3	4	5
4.	We gain new knowledge and skills through staff development and professional reading.	1	2	3	4	5
5.	We share new ideas and strategies we have gained with each other.	1	2	3	4	5
6.	Teachers at my school are supportive of each other personally and professionally.	1	2	3	4	5
7.	Teachers at my school are engaged in gaining new knowledge and skills.	1	2	3	4	5
	Enter the total of items 1–7 in the space to the right	Total Items 1–7 ____				
8.	The administrators at my school have confidence in me.	1	2	3	4	5
9.	My professional skills and competence are recognized by the administrators at my school.	1	2	3	4	5
10.	Other teachers recognize my professional skills and competence.	1	2	3	4	5
11.	It is apparent that many of the teachers at my school can take leadership roles.	1	2	3	4	5
12.	The ideas and opinions of teachers are valued and respected at my school.	1	2	3	4	5
13.	At my school we celebrate each others' successes.	1	2	3	4	5
14.	Many of the faculty and staff at my school are recognized for their work.	1	2	3	4	5
	Enter the total of items 8–14 in the space to the right	Total Items 8–14 ____				
15.	In my role as a teacher, I am free to make judgements about what is best for my students.	1	2	3	4	5
16.	At my school I have the freedom to make choices about the use of time and resources.	1	2	3	4	5

Teacher Leadership School Survey, Page 2
Respond to the following statements
in terms of how frequently each statements
is descriptive of your school.

	Never	Rarely	Some-times	Often	Always

		Never	Rarely	Sometimes	Often	Always
17.	I know that we will bend the rules if it is necessary to help children learn.	1	2	3	4	5
18.	Teachers are encouraged to take initiative to make improvements for students.	1	2	3	4	5
19.	I have input to developing a vision for my school and its future.	1	2	3	4	5
20.	At my school teachers can be innovative if they choose to be.	1	2	3	4	5
21.	Administrators and other teachers support me in making changes in my instructional strategies.	1	2	3	4	5
Enter the total of items 15–21 in the space to the right		Total Items 15–21 _____				
22.	Teachers at my school discuss strategies and share materials.	1	2	3	4	5
23.	Teachers at my school influence one another's teaching.	1	2	3	4	5
24.	Teachers in my school observe one another's work with students.	1	2	3	4	5
25.	I talk with other teachers in my school about my teaching and the curriculum.	1	2	3	4	5
26.	Teachers and administrators work together to solve students' academic and behavior problems.	1	2	3	4	5
27.	Other teachers at my school have helped me find creative ways to deal with challenges I have faced in my classes.	1	2	3	4	5
28.	Conversations among professionals at my school are focused on students.	1	2	3	4	5
Enter the total of items 22–28 in the space to the right		Total Items 22–28 _____				
29.	Teachers have input to decisions about school changes.	1	2	3	4	5
30.	Teachers have a say in what and how things are done.	1	2	3	4	5
31.	Teachers and administrators share decisions about how time is used and how the school is organized.	1	2	3	4	5
32.	Teachers and administrators at my school understand and use the consensus process.	1	2	3	4	5
33.	Teachers participate in screeing and selecting new faculty and/or staff at my school.	1	2	3	4	5
34.	My opinions and ideas are sought by administrators at my school.	1	2	3	4	5
35.	We try to each consensus before making important decisions.	1	2	3	4	5

(Continued)

Figure B.1 (Continued)

Teacher Leadership School Survey, Page 3
Respond to the following statements in terms
of how frequently each statement is descriptive of your
school.

	Never	Rarely	Some-times	Often	Always

Enter the total of items 29–35 in the space to the right	Total Items 29–35 _____
36. Because teachers and administrators share ideas about our work, I stay aware of what is happening.	[1] [2] [3] [4] [5]
37. At my school everybody talks freely and openly about feeling and opinions they have.	[1] [2] [3] [4] [5]
38. Faculty and staff at my school share their feelings and concerns in productive ways.	[1] [2] [3] [4] [5]
39. Teachers at my school discuss and help one another solve problems.	[1] [2] [3] [4] [5]
40. Faculty and staff talk about ways to better serve our students and their families.	[1] [2] [3] [4] [5]
41. When things go wrong at our school, we try not to blame, but talk about ways to do better the next time.	[1] [2] [3] [4] [5]
42. Faculty meeting time is used for discussions and problem solving.	[1] [2] [3] [4] [5]
Enter the total of items 36–42 in the space to the right	Total Items 36–42 _____
43. Teachers are treated as professionals at my school.	[1] [2] [3] [4] [5]
44. Teachers at my school look forward to coming to work every day.	[1] [2] [3] [4] [5]
45. There is a general satisfaction with the work environment among teachers at my school.	[1] [2] [3] [4] [5]
46. Teachers and administrators at my school work in partnership.	[1] [2] [3] [4] [5]
47. Teachers at my school are respected by parents, students and administrators.	[1] [2] [3] [4] [5]
48. The principal, faculty, and staff at my school work as a team.	[1] [2] [3] [4] [5]
49. We feel positive about the ways we are responding to our students' needs.	[1] [2] [3] [4] [5]
Enter the total of items 43–49 in the space to the right	Total Items 43–49 _____

Scales of the Teacher Leadership School Survey

Developmental Focus: Teachers are assisted in gaining new knowledge and skills and are encouraged to help others learn. Teachers are provided with needed assistance, guidance and coaching.

Recognition: Teachers are recognized for roles they take and the contributions they make. A spirit of mutual respect and caring exists among teachers. There are processes for the recognition of effective work.

Autonomy: Teachers are encouraged to be proactive in making improvements and innovations. Barriers are removed and resources are found to support teachers' efforts.

Collegiality: Teachers collaborate on instructional and student-related matters. Examples of collegial behavior include teachers discussing strategies, sharing materials, or observing in one another's classrooms.

Participation: Teachers are actively involved in making decisions and having input on important matters. Department chairpersons, team leaders, and other key leaders are selected with the participation of teachers.

Open Communication: Teachers send and receive information relevant to the effective functioning of the school in open, honest ways. Teachers feel informed about what is happening in the school. Teachers easily share opinions and feelings. Teachers are not blamed when things go wrong.

Positive Environment: There is general satisfaction with the work environment. Teachers feel respected by one another, by parents, students and administrators. Teachers perceive the school as having effective administrative leadership. Appointed or informal teams work together effectively in the interests of students.

Self-Scoring Procedure

✓ **Developmental Focus:**
Enter Total of Items 1–7

✓ **Recognition:**
Enter Total of Items 8–14

✓ **Autonomy:**
Enter Total of Items 15–21

✓ **Collegiality:**
Enter Total of Items 22–28

✓ **Participation:**
Enter Total of Items 29–35

✓ **Open Communication:**
Enter Total of 36–42

✓ **Positive Environment:**
Enter Total of 43–49

Teacher Leadership School Survey
For each Scale blacken the box for your score, then draw a line back to the scale name.

Scale Name	1	5	10	15	20	25	30	35	40
Developmental Focus									
Recognition									
Autonomy									
Collegiality									
Participation									
Open Communication									
Positive Environment									

Resource C

Time for Teacher Leadership

As we work with groups of educators in change efforts and ask them to identify the obstacles they face, the first response is always the new four-letter word: TIME. Similarly, the educational literature reflects the struggle teacher leaders face with time.

Time is needed for professional development along with follow-up and coaching, for teacher leaders to engage in collaborative relationships, for extensive planning for differentiated instruction to assure all students can learn, and for performing leadership responsibilities.

If we recognize that teacher leadership is a valuable contribution to school improvement, then we must acknowledge that the work takes time. Teacher leaders need time to mentor colleagues, time to complete paperwork, time to write grants to access resources for the school, and time to collaborate with other teacher leaders. As efficient as teacher leaders are, there is only so much time during the day to complete these responsibilities.

Assessing Use of Time

We suggest that school staffs complete the *Constraints of Time Inventory* (Figure C.1). This instrument will help teacher leaders and their administrators determine what their school is doing now to address time constraints. The higher the score on the instrument, the more ready the faculty is to be serious about the use of finding strategies to modify the use of time in the school.

Figure C.1   Constraints of Time Inventory

Directions: One of the main obstacles to making changes in teaching and learning in our schools is the constraint of time. Read the following items and assess the extent to which your leadership team has dealt with time as you attempted to make changes.

Scale: 4 = Accomplished
          3 = Working on this
          2 = Discussed as a possibility
          1 = No action at this time

_____ 1. Our leadership team/faculty has examined what we are doing and has abandoned programs or practices that are not improving teaching and learning in our school.

_____ 2. Our leadership team/faculty has reallocated priorities so that we have more time and resources to support our focus on improving teaching and learning in our school.

_____ 3. Our action plans include a realistic time frame for making changes at our school.

_____ 4. We have devoted portions of faculty meetings, or department or team meetings, or in-service time to helping our faculty understand the changes the leadership team has been learning about.

_____ 5. Members of the leadership team/faculty have found time to work with other teachers on the changes we want to make in teaching and learning.

_____ 6. Common planning time exists for groups of teachers in our school who need to work together on in teaching and learning.

_____ 7. We have been able to provide time outside the classroom during the school day for teachers to work on changes to curriculum, instruction, and assessment through the use of substitutes, volunteers, or existing personnel in the school, or other means.

_____ 8. We have created time by using faculty meetings, staff development days, or grade or department meetings differently.

_____ 9. We have found ways to make better use of our time through the use of the computer or other technology.

_____ 10. We have reduced wasted time through planning and facilitating more efficient meetings.

_____ **TOTAL**

Strategies for Finding Time

Innovative schools across the country have found ways to move beyond tradition to build new time structures. Listed below are some suggested strategies that may be considered by individual schools.

Better-Used Time

We often use existing time ineffectively. Listed below are strategies that may help with this problem.

- Use faculty meetings for professional learning rather than for dealing with administrative procedures.
- Use Web sites, e-mail, or text messaging to disseminate information, eliminating unnecessary large group meetings.
- Ask a faculty member to facilitate a single-issue faculty meeting in order to consider a schoolwide issue in depth.
- Create a wiki to communicate among teachers and to enable teachers to provide input in an easily accessible way.
- Rather than evaluating all teachers every year, use professional growth plans for competent teachers and evaluate once every three years.
- Annually, consider if all the regularly scheduled meetings are really necessary. Vigorously question the accomplishments of the time spent in the meetings, and eliminate unnecessary meetings.
- Assure that facilitation skills are learned by all faculty members to make meetings more effective and efficient.
- Provide each teacher with a cell phone to allow for efficiency in parent contacts.
- Empower teachers to modify designated district professional development days and to restructure the time to meet individual schools' needs. For example, schedule two-hour blocks more frequently to reinforce or problem solve during a new program implementation.
- Utilize videoconferencing to save teachers time in traveling to district-level meetings away from the school site.
- Coordinate professional development within the school, the feeder schools, and the school district to take advantage of resources that may be too expensive for one school or teacher.
- Critically examine procedures, programs, and paperwork to purposefully abandon unnecessary work. Find volunteers on

the staff to form a task force to work on this problem and make recommendations for abandonment of inefficiencies.

- Audiotape important information (e.g., superintendent messages, recent court decisions, new resources) for teachers to listen to during their commutes.

Freed-Up Time

This category of strategies uses existing or free resources to relieve teachers from regular duties with direct student contact.

- Find ways to authorize qualified staff (administrators, support staff, district office personnel) to cover classes for teachers.
- Engage parents or volunteers to read to students for short periods or work in small groups with students to allow teachers time for collaborative endeavors.
- Ask team teachers to pool students so that some members of the team can be released for collaborative work, planning, or development opportunities.
- Combine classes for a special event to free teachers. A partnership with a community theater could provide performances for the students, or secondary students could engage in community service activities.
- Build a partnership with local business people, and engage them in providing enrichment experiences for the students while the teachers are learning together.
- Partner with a local university forming a professional development school, and utilize student interns and university professors in leading classes while teachers meet to share and learn.
- Design a theme day for three grade levels so that on selected afternoons, teachers of two of the grade levels can be released for work together.
- Give students higher-order thinking independent study assignments that require them to use resources outside the classroom setting, such as the media center with supervision provided by the media center personnel.

Common Time

Teachers who share common students and the same planning time have opportunities for working together that are impossible otherwise.

Offer teachers involved in new initiatives (e.g., implementation of new math curriculum or teaching a new course) a common time to meet and learn from one another about their experiences utilizing classroom coverage by substitutes or administrators. Set up a listserv for these teachers to communicate frequently between face-to-face meetings.

- Organize academic teachers into teams and provide each team with a common planning period for sharing information, collaborating on projects, or doing action research that benefits the whole team.
- Give each individual subject area a daily common planning time.
- Arrange the master schedule to allow for a common planning period at least biweekly for each grade level team.
- Schedule electives or special subjects before or after lunch or at the end of the day to enable teachers to have shared learning time, which may be extended if they choose.
- Utilize collaborative software to allow teachers to hold synchronous chats with teachers from other school sites; this can be especially helpful for those teachers who do not have subject area colleagues within the building.
- Pair a new teacher with an experienced teacher at the same grade level or in the same subject area, and offer occasional common time for mentoring, sharing, and advising. Utilize district staff personnel to teach their classes or to model lessons that both teachers observe and later discuss.

Restructured Time

In this strategy, the school staff uses the existing allocated time and restructures or reschedules it.

- Use block scheduling, which is common in secondary schools, and vary the use of block time depending on the needs of the students.
- Continuously evaluate the organization of the school day to identify or organize time for teacher learning. Change the schedule if needed rather than waiting until the next school year.
- Design the school day so that teachers, especially at the secondary level, do not have to meet the students every day. Use larger classes occasionally for special topics, films, or projects.

- Consider year-round calendars for schooling, which provide concentrated time for intensive professional development during intercessions between quarters.
- Ask teachers to "bank" time for extended time to work together.
- Delay arrival time for students, and create a first period in which teachers work together when they have a higher level of energy.
- Consider designing smaller schools within a school or learning communities, which allow for more flexibility in scheduling students.
- Add time to the students' day on four days so that they are released on the fifth day.
- Coordinate with community agencies, such as churches or synagogues, scouts, or other organizations to provide activities at the times scheduled for early release of students.
- Make a trade-off with teachers. If they meet on Saturday or after school, grant them released time on a regular professional development day.
- When "required" professional development is necessary for the whole faculty or a specific group of teachers, provide options for their participation (e.g., before school, after school, at planning times, or via distance learning that can be accessed from teachers' homes).

Purchased Time

Finding time for teachers to assume leadership roles demands resources. Common strategies that require fiscal resources include the following:

- Invest resources in an extra teaching position in the building to be used as a rotating substitute teacher who can free teachers when time is needed.
- Provide a personal digital assistant (PDA) for each teacher to use for storing student or parent contact information, e-mail communication with other faculty members, Web research, or virtually accessing university courses.
- Extend the teacher contract into weeks when students are on vacation to allow for long-range planning, learning new skills, and collaborative design of new programs. For intensive work and learning together, a minimum of two weeks is needed.
- Allow two teacher leaders who are heavily involved in a reform effort to share one teaching position between them, releasing each for leadership work when the other is in the classroom.

- Solicit and write grants to support time for teacher leadership. Most granting institutions now look for professional development time to be built into a grant to help ensure that the project will be successful.
- While paying attention to student needs, consider ways to modify class sizes; the addition of one or two students to each class can provide the funds for hiring teams of substitutes who can cover classes occasionally. This helps support continuity of learning by calming anxious parents who want the "real" teacher in the classroom and relieving teacher guilt for being away from the students.
- Organize administrators and substitutes who could come into a school and take over the school for a full day to release faculty and staff for intensive planning.
- Place more resources (e.g., clerical help, volunteers, aides, assistants) at the classroom level to increase instructional support for the teacher in order to provide more time.
- Obtain stipends for teachers to attend professional development during the summer.
- Offer recertification credit for teacher leadership responsibilities that involve learning, such as curriculum revision to meet new standards.
- Invest in technology that can be used to provide alternate ways for teachers to meet and collaborate.

Resource D

Teacher Leadership Books, Instruments, and Organizations

If you want to pursue your interest in teacher leadership, you may want to examine the following materials. These will lead you to other resources as you continue to explore teacher leadership.

Books

Leadership

Barth, R. S. (2001). *Learning by heart*. San Francisco: Jossey-Bass.

Byrk, A. S., & Schneider, B. (2002). *Trust in schools: A core resource for improvement*. New York: Russell Sage Foundation.

Chrispeels, J. H. (Ed.). (2004). *Learning to lead together: The promise and challenge of sharing leadership*. Thousand Oaks, CA: Sage Publications.

Donaldson, G. A. (2006). *Cultivating leadership in schools: Connecting people, purpose, and practice* (2nd ed.). New York: Teachers College Press.

Heifetz, R. A., & Linsky, M. (2002). *Leadership on the line: Staying alive through the dangers of leading*. Boston: Harvard Business School Press.

Jennings, M. (2007). *Leading effective meetings, teams, and work groups in districts and schools*. Alexandria, VA: Association for Supervision and Curriculum Development.

Whitaker, T. (2002). *Dealing with difficult teachers* (2nd ed.). Larchmont, NY: Eye on Education.

Professional Learning

Drago-Severson, E. (2004). *Helping teachers learn: Principal leadership for adult growth and development*. Thousand Oaks, CA: Corwin.

Easton, L. B. (2008). *Powerful designs for professional learning* (2nd ed.). Oxford, OH: National Staff Development Council.

Guskey, T. (1999). *Evaluating professional development*. Thousand Oaks, CA: Corwin.

Loucks-Horsley, S., Love, N., Stiles, K. E., Mundry, S. E., & Hewson, P. W. (2003). *Designing professional development for teachers of science and mathematics* (2nd ed.). Thousand Oaks, CA: Corwin.

Jolly, A. (2008). *Team to teach: A facilitator's guide to professional learning teams*. National Staff Development Council.

Zepeda, S. J. (2008). *Professional development: What works*. Larchmont, NY: Eye on Education.

Teacher Leadership

Ackerman, R. H., & Mackenzie, S. V. (Eds.). (2007). *Uncovering teacher leadership: Essays and voices from the field*. Thousand Oaks, CA: Corwin.

Crowther, F., with Ferguson, M., & Hann, L. (2008). *Developing teacher leaders: How teacher leadership enhances school success* (2nd ed.). Thousand Oaks, CA: Corwin.

Gabriel, J. G. (2005). *How to thrive as a teacher leader*. Alexandria, VA: Association for Supervision and Curriculum Development.

Harris, A., & Muijs, D. (2004). *Improving schools through teacher leadership*. Maidenhead, Berkshire, UK: Open University Press.

Killion, J., & Harrison, C. (2006). *Taking the lead: New roles for teachers and school-based coaches*. Oxford, OH: National Staff Development Council.

Lieberman, A., & Miller, L. (2004). *Teacher leadership*. San Francisco, CA: Jossey-Bass.

Mangin, M. M., & Stoelinga, S. R. (2008). *Effective teacher leadership: Using research to inform and reform*. New York: Teachers College Press.

Moller, G., & Pankake, A. (2006). *Lead with me: A principal's guide to teacher leadership*. Larchmont, NY: Eye on Education.

Reeves, D. B. (2008). *Reframing teacher leadership to improve your school*. Alexandria, VA: Association for Supervision and Curriculum Development.

Troen, V., & Boles, K. (2003). *Who's teaching your children? Why the teacher crisis is worse than you think and what can be done about it*. New Haven, CT: Yale University Press.

Instruments

Assessing Your Readiness for Teacher Leadership®
Teacher Leadership School Survey®
Teacher Leadership Self Assessment®
Professional Development Center, Inc.
P.O. Box 46609
Tampa, FL 33647
Telephone: (813) 991–5101
E-mail: mkatzen383@aol.com

Philosophy of Education Inventory®
Lifelong Learning Options
420 South 12th Street, Suite 107
Quincy, IL 62301–4304 USA
Telephone: (217) 221–5466
Fax: (217) 228–5504
E-mail: lifelong.order@ecentral.com

Organizations

Association for Supervision and Curriculum Development
1703 North Beauregard Street
Alexandria, VA 22311-1714
Telephone: (703) 578-9600
Fax: (703) 575-5400
Internet: http://www.ascd.org

Center for Teaching Quality
Teacher Leaders Network (http://www.teacherleaders.org)
500 Millstone Drive, Suite 102
Hillsborough, NC 27278
Telephone: (919) 241-1575
Fax: (919) 241-1576
Internet: http://www.teachingquality.org

National Board for Professional Teaching Standards
1525 Wilson Boulevard, Suite 500
Arlington, VA 22209
Telephone: (800) 22-TEACH ((800) 228-3224)
Internet: http://www.nbpts.org

National School Reform Faculty
Harmony Education Center
P.O. Box 1787
Bloomington, IN 47402
Telephone: (812) 330-2702
Fax: (812) 333-3435
Internet: http://nsrfharmonyschool.org

National Staff Development Council
P.O. Box 240
Oxford, OH 45056
Telephone: (800) 727-7288
Internet: http://www.nsdc.org

References

Ackerman, R. H., & Mackenzie, S. V. (Eds.). (2007). *Uncovering teacher leadership: Essays and voices from the field.* Thousand Oaks, CA: Corwin.

Anderson, C. S. (1992). The search for school climate: A review of the research. *Review of Educational Research, 52*(3), 368–420.

Badaracco, J. L., Jr. (2002). *Leading quietly.* Cambridge, MA: Harvard Business School Press.

Baratz-Snowden, J. (2007). *The future of teacher compensation: Déjà vu or something new?* Washington, DC: Center for American Progress. Retrieved November 8, 2008, from http://www.americanprogress.org/issues/2007/11/pdf/snowden_report.pdf

Barth, R. S. (1988). School: A community of leaders. In A. Lieberman (Ed.), *Building a professional culture in schools* (pp. 129–147). New York: Teachers College Press.

Barth, R. S. (2001). Teacher leader. *Phi Delta Kappan, 82*(6), 443–449.

Barth, R. S. (2006). Improving relationships within the schoolhouse. *Educational Leadership, 63*(6), 9–13.

Barth, R. S. (2007). The teacher leader. In R. H. Ackerman & S. V. Mackenzie (Eds.), *Uncovering teacher leadership: Essays and voices from the field* (pp. 9–36). Thousand Oaks, CA: Corwin.

Beachum, F., & Dentith, A. (2004). Teacher leaders creating cultures of school renewal and transformation. *The Educational Forum, 68*(3), 276–286.

Berg, J. H. (2007). *Resources for reform: The role of board-certified teachers in improving the quality of teaching.* Unpublished doctoral dissertation, Harvard University, Cambridge, MA.

Berry, B., Norton, J., & Byrd, A. (2007). Lessons from networking. *Educational Leadership, 65*(1), 48–52.

Blasé, J., & Blasé, J. (1997). The micropolitical orientation of facilitative school principals and its effects on teachers' sense of empowerment. *Journal of Educational Administration, 35*(2), 138–164.

Boyer, E. L. (1983). *High school.* New York: Harper & Row.

Calhoun, E. (2002). Action research for school improvement. *Educational Leadership, 59*(6), 18–24.

Carlson, H. C. (2004). Changing of the guard: A new generation of teacher leaders will raise quality-of-life priorities. *The School Administrator, 61*(7), 36–39.

Caro-Bruce, C., Flessner, R., Klehr, M., & Zeichner, K. (2007). *Creating equitable classrooms through action research*. Thousand Oaks, CA: Corwin.

Carnegie Forum on Education and the Economy. (1986). *A nation prepared: Teachers for the 21st century. The report of the task force on the teaching profession*. New York: Author.

Center for Teaching Quality. (2007). *Performance-pay for teachers: Designing a system that students deserve*. Hillsborough, NC: Author.

Center for Teaching Quality. (2008). *Data and recommendations matrix*. Hillsborough, NC: Author. Retrieved November 13, 2008, from http:// www.teacherworkingconditions.org/dataanalysis/matrix.html

Chait, R. (2007). *Current state policies that reform teacher pay: An examination of pay-for-performance programs in eight states*. Washington, DC: Center for American Progress.

Cochran-Smith, M. (2006). *Stayers, leavers, lovers, and dreamers: Why people teach and why they stay* (2004 Barbara Biber Lecture. Occasional Paper Series 16). New York: Bank Street College of Education.

Cochran-Smith, M., & Lytle, S. L. (2006). Troubling images of teaching in No Child Left Behind. *Harvard Educational Review, 76*(4), 668–697.

Cotton, K. (2003). *Principals and student achievement: What the research says*. Alexandria, VA: Association for Supervision and Curriculum Development.

Coyle, M. (1997). Teacher leadership vs. school management: Flatten the hierarchies. *Clearing House, 70*, 236–239.

Crowther, F., with Ferguson, M., & Hann, L. (2008). *Developing teacher leaders: How teacher leadership enhances school success* (2nd ed.). Thousand Oaks, CA: Corwin.

Danielson, C. (2007). The many faces of leadership. *Educational Leadership, 65*(1), 14–19.

Darling-Hammond, L. (1997). *Right to learn*. San Francisco: Jossey-Bass.

Darling-Hammond, L., & Prince, C. D. (2007). *Strengthening teacher quality in high-need schools—policy and practice*. Washington, DC: Council of Chief State School Officers.

Dittman, M. (2005). Generational differences at work. *Monitor on Psychology, 36*(6), 54. Retrieved March 3, 2008, from http://www.apa.org/monitor/ jun05/generational.html

Donaldson, G. A. (2006). *Cultivating leadership in schools: Connecting people, purpose, and practice* (2nd ed.). New York: Teachers College Press.

Donaldson, M. L., Johnson, S. M., Kirkpatrick, C. L., Marinell, W. H., Steele, J. L., & Szczesiul, S. A. (2008). Angling for access, bartering for change: How second-stage teachers experience differentiated roles in schools. *Teachers College Record, 110*(5), 1088–1114.

Drago-Severson, E. (2004). *Helping teachers learn: Principal leadership for adult growth and development*. Thousand Oaks, CA: Corwin.

Du, F. (2007). A case study of teacher leaders as group leaders: Implications for research and teacher education. *The Teacher Educator, 42*(3), 185–208.

DuFour, R. (2004). What is a professional learning community? *Educational Leadership, 61*(8), 6–11.

Education Commission of the States. (2000). *In pursuit of quality teaching: Five key strategies for policy makers*. Denver, CO: Author.

Education Week. (2008). *Quality counts 2008: Tapping into teaching: Unlocking the key to student success.* Bethesda, MD: Author.

Farkas, S., Foley P., & Duffett, A., with Foleno, T., & Johnson, J. (2001*). Just waiting to be asked: A fresh look at attitudes on public engagement.* New York: Public Agenda. Retrieved April 17, 2008, from http://www.publicagenda.org/specials/pubengage/pubengage.htm

Ferren, C. (2000). Become a leader by taking responsibility every day. *The Journal for Quality and Participation, 23*(1). Retrieved December 6, 2007, from http://0-web.ebscohost.com.wncln.wncln.org/ehost/pdf?vid=3&hid=115&sid=8dda2d0d-4a71–48db-ba1d-79cb40978d4e%40sessionmgr106

Fullan, M. G. (2005). *Leadership and sustainability: System thinkers in action.* Thousand Oaks, CA: Corwin.

Gabriel, J. G. (2005). *How to thrive as a teacher leader.* Alexandria, VA: Association for Supervision and Curriculum Development.

Goldring, E. B., & Rallis, S. F. (1993). *Principals of dynamic schools: Taking charge of change.* Newbury Park, CA: Corwin.

Goodlad, J. (1990). The occupation of teaching in schools. In J. Goodlad & R. Soder (Eds.), *The moral dimensions of teaching* (pp. 33–34). San Francisco: Jossey-Bass.

Hall, G. E., & Hord, S. M. (1987). *Change in schools: Facilitating the process.* Albany: State University of New York Press.

Hargreaves, A., & Fink, D. (2004). The seven principles of sustainable leadership. *Educational Leadership, 61*(7), 8–15.

Hargreaves, A., & Fullan, M. G. (1996). *What's worth fighting for in your school?* New York: Teachers College Press.

Hargreaves, A., & Fullan, M. G. (1998). *What's worth fighting for out there?* New York: Teachers College Press.

Harris, A., & Spillane, J. (2008). Distributed leadership through the looking glass. *Management in Education, 22*(1), 31–34.

Harris, B. (2003). *Noel Tichy: Leadership beyond vision.* Missoula: Montana Associated Technologies Roundtables. Retrieved December 6, 2007, from http://www.matr.net/article-9269.html

Hart, A. W. (1990). Impacts of the school social unit on teacher authority during work redesign. *American Educational Research Journal, 27,* 503–532.

Hart, P., & Segesta, J. (1994). *Leadership development for teachers: 1994 evaluation.* Tampa, FL: West Central Educational Leadership Network.

Hawley, W. D., & Valli, L. (1999). The essentials of effective professional development: A new consensus. In L. Darling-Hammond & G. Sykes (Eds.), *Teaching as the learning profession: Handbook of policy and practice* (pp. 127–150). San Francisco: Jossey-Bass.

Heller, M. F., & Firestone, W. A. (1994). *Heroes, teams, and teachers: A study of leadership for change.* (ERIC Document Reproduction Service, No. ED).

Heneman, H. G. III, & Milanowski, A. T. (2004). Alignment of human resource practices and teacher performance competency. *Peabody Journal of Education, 79*(4), 108–125.

Heneman, H. G. III, Milanowski, A. T., Kimball, S. M., & Odden, A. (2006). *Standards-based teacher evaluation as a foundation for knowledge- and skill-based pay* (CPRE Policy Brief RB-45). Philadelphia, PA: Consortium for Policy Research in Education.

Hersey, P., & Natemeyer, W. E. (1979). *Power perception profile*. Escondido, CA: Center for Leadership Studies.

Hewitt-Gervais, C. M. (1996). *Summary of evaluations: Leadership development for teachers*. Tampa, FL: West Central Educational Leadership Network.

Hirsch, E., & Emerick S., with Church, K., & Fuller, E. (2006a). *Arizona teacher working conditions: Designing schools for educator and student success*. Hillsborough, NC: Center for Teaching Quality. Retrieved December 8, 2007, from http://www.teachingquality.org/pdfs/twcaz2006.pdf

Hirsch, E., Emerick, S. Church, K., & Fuller, E. (2006b). *Teacher working conditions are student learning conditions: A report on the 2006 North Carolina Teacher Working Conditions Survey*. Hillsborough, NC: Center for Teaching Quality.

Hord, S. (2003). Introduction. In S. Hord (Ed.), *Learning together, leading together: Changing schools through professional learning communities* (pp. 1–14). New York: Teachers College Press.

Ingersoll, R. M. (2007). Short on power, long on responsibility. *Educational Leadership, 65*(1), 20–25.

Ingersoll, R. M., & Smith, T. M. (2003). The wrong solution to the teacher shortage. *Educational Leadership, 60*(8), 30–33.

Institute for Educational Leadership. (2001). *Leadership for student learning: Redefining the teacher as leader*. Washington, DC: Author. Retrieved July 31, 2005, from http://www.iel.org/pubs/sl21ci.html

Johnson, S. M., & Donaldson, M. L. (2007). Overcoming obstacles to leadership. *Educational Leadership, 65*(1), 8–13.

Katzenmeyer, W., & Katzenmeyer, M. (2004). *Teacher leader self assessment*. Tampa, FL: Professional Development Center.

Katzenmeyer, W., & Katzenmeyer, M. (2005). *Teacher leader school survey*. Tampa, FL: Professional Development Center.

King, B., Louis, K. S., Marks, H. M., & Peterson, K. D. (1996). Participatory decision making. In F. Newmann (Ed.), *Authentic assessment: Restructuring schools for intellectual quality* (pp. 245–263). San Francisco: Jossey-Bass.

Lambert, L. (1998). *Building leadership capacity in schools*. Alexandria, VA: Association for Supervision and Curriculum Development.

Lambert, L. (2002). A framework for shared leadership. *Educational Leadership, 59*(8), 37–40.

Lambert, L. (2003). *Leadership capacity for lasting school improvement*. Alexandria, VA: Association for Supervision and Curriculum Development.

Lancaster, L., & Stillman, D. (2002). *When generations collide who they are. Why they clash. How to solve the generational puzzle at work*. New York: HarperCollins.

Lanier, J. & Darling-Hammond, L. (2005). *Professional development schools: Schools for developing a profession*. New York: Teachers College Press.

Leithwood, K. A. (1992). The principal's role in teacher development. In M. Fullan & A. Hargreaves (Eds.), *Teacher development and educational change* (pp. 56–85). Bristol, PA: Falmer.

Lezotte, L. E., & Jacoby, B. C. (1990). *A guide to the school improvement process based on effective schools research*. Okemos, MI: Effective Schools Products.

Lieberman, A., & Miller, L. (1999). *Teachers: Transforming their world and their work*. New York: Teachers College Press.

Lieberman, A., & Miller, L. (2004). *Teacher leadership*. San Francisco: Jossey-Bass

Lieberman, A., & Wood, D. (2003). *Inside the National Writing Project: Connecting network learning and classroom teaching.* New York: Teachers College Press.

Little, J. W. (1993). Teachers' professional development in a climate of educational reform. *Educational Evaluation and Policy Analysis, 15,* 129–151.

Little, J. W. (1995). Contested ground: The basis of teacher leadership in two restructuring high schools. *Elementary School Journal, 96*(1), 47–73.

Little, J. W. (1996). The emotional contours and career trajectories of (disappointed) reform enthusiasts. *Cambridge Journal of Education, 26,* 345–359.

Lortie, D. C. (1975). *Schoolteacher: A sociological study of teaching.* Chicago: University of Chicago Press.

Louis, K. S., & Marks, H. (1996). *Does professional community affect the classroom? Teachers' work and student experiences in restructuring schools.* Paper presented at the annual meeting of the American Educational Research Association, New York.

Mackenzie, S. V. (2007). (How) can a new vision of teacher leadership be fulfilled? In R. H. Ackerman & S. V. Mackenzie (Eds.), *Uncovering teacher leadership: Essays and voices from the field* (pp. 373–382). Thousand Oaks, CA: Corwin.

Maeroff, G. I. (1988). Teacher empowerment: A step toward professionalization. *NASSP Bulletin, 72*(511), 52–60.

Mangin, M. M. (2005). *Distributed leadership and the teacher leader: Teachers' perspectives.* Paper presented at the annual meeting of the American Educational Research Association, Montreal, Canada.

Mangin, M. M., & Stoelinga S. R. (2008). Teacher leadership: What it is and why it matters. In M. M. Mangin & S. R. Stoelinga (Eds.), *Effective teacher leadership: Using research to inform and reform* (pp. 1–9). New York: Teachers College Press.

McLaughlin, M., & Talbert, J. (2001) *Professional communities and the work of high school teaching.* Chicago: University of Chicago Press.

Moller, G., & Pankake, A. (2006). *Lead with me: A principal's guide to teacher leadership.* Larchmont, NY: Eye on Education.

Moller, G., Pankake, A., Huffman, J. B., Hipp, K. A., Cowan, D., & Oliver, D. (2000). *Teacher leadership: A product of supportive & shared leadership within professional learning communities.* Paper presented at the annual meeting of the American Educational Research Association, New Orleans, LA.

Mooney, T. (1994). *Teachers as leaders: Hope for the future.* Washington, DC: National Commission on Excellence in Education. (ERIC Document Reproduction Service, No. ED 380407).

National Board for Professional Teaching Standards. (2008a). *Better teaching, better learning, better schools.* Retrieved January 27, 2009, from http://www.nbpts.org/

National Board for Professional Teaching Standards. (2008b). *The five core propositions.* Retrieved August 5, 2008, from http://www.nbpts.org/the_standards/the_five_core_propositio

National Commission for Teaching and America's Future. (2007). *Policy brief: The high cost of teacher turnover.* Washington, DC: Author.

National Institute for Excellence in Teaching. (2007). *Creating a successful performance compensation system for educators.* Santa Monica, CA: Author. Retrieved November 8, 2008, from http://www.talentedteachers.org/pubs/successful_performance_pay_july_2007.pdf

Newmann, F. M., & Wehlage, G. G. (1995). *Successful school restructuring: A report to the public and educators.* Madison: Center on Organization and Restructuring of Schools, Wisconsin Center for Education Research, University of Wisconsin.

North Carolina State Board of Education. (2005.) *North Carolina State Board of Education policy manual* (Policy ID Number: QP-A-005). Raleigh, NC: Author. Retrieved April 8, 2008, from http://www.ncpublicschools.org/sbe_meetings/0505/0505_QP.pdf

O'Connor, K., & Boles, K. (1992). *Assessing the needs of teacher leaders in Massachusetts.* Paper presented at the annual meeting of the American Educational Research Association, San Francisco, CA.

Ovando, M. N. (1994). *Effects of teachers' leadership on their teaching practices.* Paper presented at the annual conference of the University Council of Educational Administration, Philadelphia, PA.

Patterson, J. L. (1993). *Leadership for tomorrow's schools.* Alexandria, VA: Association for Supervision and Curriculum Development.

Peterson, K. D., & Deal, T. E. (1998). How leaders influence the culture of schools. *Educational Leadership, 56*(1), 28–30.

Resnick, L. B., & Hall, M. W. (1998). Learning organizations for sustainable education reform. *Daedalus, 127*(4), 89–117.

Rosenholtz, S. J. (1989). *Teachers' workplace: The social organization of schools.* New York: Longman.

Sagor, R. (2004). *The action research guidebook: A four-step process for educators and school teams.* Thousand Oaks, CA: Corwin.

Schaubroeck, J., Ganster, D. C., & Kemmerer, B. (1996). Does trait promote stability? *Journal of Organizational Behavior, 19*(2), 191–196.

Schön, D. A. (1995). *The reflective practitioner: How professionals think in action* (new ed.). Burlington, VT: Ashgate.

Sergiovanni, T. J. (2000). *Leadership for the schoolhouse: How is it different? Why is it important?* San Francisco: Jossey-Bass.

Shen, J. (1998). Do teachers feel empowered? *Educational Leadership, 55*(7), 35–36.

Sherrill, J. A. (1999). Preparing teachers for leadership roles in the 21st century. *Theory Into Practice, 38,* 56–61.

Silva, D. Y., Gimbert, B., & Nolan, J. (2000). Sliding the doors: Locking and unlocking possibilities for teacher leadership. *Teachers College Record, 102*(4), 779–803.

Slotnik, W. J. (2005). Mission possible: Tying earning to learning. *Education Week,* 32–33, 40.

Smylie, M. A., & Denny, J. W. (1990). Teacher leadership: Tensions and ambiguities in organizational perspectives. *Educational Administration Quarterly, 26,* 235–259.

Snell, J., & Swanson, J. (2000). *The essential knowledge and skills of teacher leaders: A search for a conceptual framework.* Paper presented at the annual meeting of the American Education Research Association, New Orleans, LA.

Southeast Center for Teaching Quality. (2002). *Teacher leadership for teaching quality: The teachers network policy institute model.* Chapel Hill, NC: Author.

Staw, B. M. (1986). Organizational psychology and the pursuit of the happy/productive worker. *California Management Review, 20*(3), 63–74.

Steffy, B. E., Wolfe, M. P., Pasch, S. H., & Enz, B. J. (Eds.). (1999). *Life cycle of the career teacher.* Thousand Oaks, CA: Corwin.

Stein, M. K. (1998). *High performance learning communities. District 2: Report on year one implementation of school learning communities.* Pittsburgh, PA: Pittsburgh University Learning and Research Center. (ERIC Document Reproduction Service, No. ED 429263).

Stein, M. K., Smith, M. S., & Silver, E. A. (1999). The development of professional developers: Learning to assist teachers in new settings in new ways. *Harvard Educational Review, 69,* 237–270.

Stone, M., Horejs, J., & Lomas, A. (1997). Commonalities and differences in teacher leadership at the elementary, middle, and high school levels. *Action in Teacher Education, 19*(3), 49–64.

Sykes, G. (1999). Teacher and student learning: Strengthening their connection. In L. Darling-Hammond & G. Sykes (Eds.), *Teaching as the learning profession: Handbook of policy and practice* (pp. 151–180). San Francisco: Jossey-Bass.

Taylor, P. G., Russ-Eft, D. F., & Chan, D. W. L. (2005). A meta-analytic review of behavior modeling training. *Journal of Applied Psychology, 90*(4), 692–709.

Teacher Advancement Program Foundation. (2005). *Understanding the Teacher Advancement Program.* Santa Monica, CA: Author.

Teacher Leader Network. (2009). *Who we are.* Retrieved January 27, 2009, from http://www.teacherleaders.org/about/who

Tichenor, M. S., & Tichenor J. M. (Fall 2004 & Winter 2005). Understanding teachers' perspectives on professionalism. *The Professional Educator, 27*(1 & 2), 89–95.

Troen, V., & Boles, K. (1994). Two teachers examine the power of teacher leadership. In D. R. Walling (Ed.), *Teachers as leaders: Perspectives on the professional development of teachers* (pp. 275-286). Bloomington, IN: Phi Delta Kappa.

Troen, V., & Boles, K. (2003). *Who's teaching your children? Why the teacher crisis is worse than you think and what can be done about it.* New Haven, CT: Yale University Press.

Viadero, D. (2008). Working conditions trump pay. *Education Week, 27*(18), pp. 32–35.

von Frank, V. (Ed.). (2008). *Finding time for professional learning.* Oxford, OH: National Staff Development Council.

Wechsler, M., Tiffany-Morales, J., Campbell, A., Humphrey, D., Kim, D., Shields, P., et al. (2007). *The status of the teaching profession 2007.* Santa Cruz, CA: The Center for the Future of Teaching and Learning.

Wehling, B. (Ed.). (2007). Foreward. In *Building a 21st century U.S. education system* (pp. 13-21). Washington, DC: National Commission on Teaching and America's Future. Retrieved February 11, 2008, from http://www.ecs.org/html/offsite.asp?document=http%3A%2F%2Fwww%2Enctaf%2Eorg%2F

Weiss, C. H., Cambone, J., & Wyeth, A. (1992). Trouble in paradise: Teacher conflicts in shared decision making. *Educational Administration Quarterly, 28,* 350–367.

Wong, H. K., & Wong, R. T. (2007). Teachers: The next generation. *ASCD Express.* Retrieved April 7, 2008, from http://www.newteacher.com/pdf/ascd_express_wong_teachers.pdf

York-Barr, J., & Duke, K. (2004). What do we know about teacher leadership? Findings from two decades of scholarship. *Review of Educational Research, 74*(3), 255–316.

Zinn, L. F. (1997). *Support and barriers to teacher leadership: Reports of teacher leaders.* Paper presented at the annual meeting of the American Educational Research Association, Chicago, IL.

Zinn, L. M. (1996). *Philosophy of education inventory.* Boulder, CO: Lifelong Learning Options.

Chapter Quotations

Chapter 1: Sacks, A. (2008). *Teacher leadership at the Ford Foundation.* Retrieved November 8, 2008, from http://teacherleaders.typepad.com/shoulders_of_giants/2008/10/teacher-leaders.html

Chapter 2: Reber, K. (2003). *Teacher leadership: Answers by Betsy Rogers.* Retrieved November 12, 2008, from http://www.teacherscount.org/teacher/topic/topic-rogers.shtml

Chapter 3: Flanagan, N. (2008). *For and by teachers.* Retrieved November 8, 2008, from http://teacherleaders.typepad.com/teacher_in_a_strange_land/teachers_as_leaders/

Chapter 4: Ferriter, B. (2008). *Tapping into your superhero . . .* Retrieved November 12, 2008, from http://teacherleaders.typepad.com/the_tempered_radical/teaching_quality

Chapter 5: Moore, R. (2008). *Teachers and administrators: Getting in step.* Retrieved November 8, 2008, from http://teacherleaders.typepad.com/teachmoore/2008/10/although-you-mi. html

Chapter 6: Teacher Leaders Network. (2005). *Teacher leaders network conversations: We need a new mental model of the successful school.* Retrieved November 12, 2008, from http://www.teacherleaders.org/node/791

Chapter 7: Graham, S. (2008). *You may say that I'm a dreamer . . .* Retrieved November 12, 2008, from http://blogs.edweek.org/teachers/place_at_the_table/2008/07/you_may_say_that_im_a_dreamer.html

Chapter 8: Center for Teaching Quality. (2008). *Improving student learning through strategic compensation: A TeacherSolutions report from the Teacher Leaders of TLN-Kansas.* Hillsborough, NC: Author. Retrieved November 10, 2008, from http://catalog.proemags.com/showmag.php?mid=ggfgt#/page17/

Index

CORWIN

A SAGE Company

The Corwin logo—a raven striding across an open book—represents the union of courage and learning. Corwin is committed to improving education for all learners by publishing books and other professional development resources for those serving the field of PreK–12 education. By providing practical, hands-on materials, Corwin continues to carry out the promise of its motto: **"Helping Educators Do Their Work Better."**